MORE THINKING ABOUT LIFE

More Thinking About Life

Published by George Bryant
bryantgw@xtra.co.nz

© 2025 George Bryant

ISBN: 978-0-473-73645-3

No part of this publication may be reproduced, stored in a retrieval system, or transmitted in any form or by any means, electronic mechanical, photocopying, recording or otherwise, without prior written permission from the author.

Production: Outline Print Consultancy

Printed in New Zealand

Dedication

To those who step off life's
treadmill long enough to
reflect on the way we live.

Thanks

I'm most grateful to all those people, both friends and strangers, who have eagerly engaged in discussions with me over a range of topics whenever and wherever we've met. Of course, we haven't always agreed but the debate has been useful and provoked much thought.

Grateful thanks also go to those who read and commented on my manuscript: my lovely wife, Joan, always a first responder; my lawyer friends Even Turbott and John Foote; writers Elaine Dixon and Adrienne Malcolmson; and former mayor of Tauranga, Greg Brownless.

I also thank my daughter, Julia Rae, for her input into the cover design, and my colleague, Andrew Killick, for his wise counsel.

Contents

A Word

PART A

1. More Thinking About Life 13
2. We're all Different 17
3. Seeking Happiness 23
4. Diminishing Empathy 29
5. We Always Want More 37
6. When the Going Gets Tough 47
7. Living With Cancer 51

PART B

8. Words Matter 65
9. How Free is Speech? 73
10. Truth Decay 85
11. Wanted – More Wisdom 93
12. Spirituality and Politics 101
13. Please Don't Call Me Racist 107
14. Is the End Really Nigh? 115
15. Is There any hope? 127

PART C

16. Adapt and Survive 135
17. Learnings From Life 139

A Word

Life's but a walking shadow, a poor player

That struts and frets his hour upon the stage

And then is heard no more. It is a tale

Told by an idiot, full of sound and fury,

Signifying nothing.[1]

This quote has been anchored in my mind ever since my student days. Macbeth is nearing the end of his life. The guilt of his murder of the King, and others, is preying upon his mind. His wife has committed suicide. His enemies are closing in.

I can fully understand why, in this situation, life might appear to be meaningless to Macbeth.

But he is wrong. Life is full of meaning, even in crisis situations. I've written about aspects of this many times, as I continue to do in this book.

True, I contemplate some of life's downsides but also its upsides. I ponder our pain in tough times, our search for happiness, the decay of truth, and even the possible collapse of civilisation, but I also look at the need for wisdom and spirituality. I rejoice in the uniqueness of human beings and the need for more compassion. I express a desire for more freedom of speech, and greater urgency combatting climate change, and I look forward in hope.

If the reader is looking for a theme, I guess it's my regard for the dignity, importance and uniqueness of individual human beings, especially those who suffer at the hands of others – the value of the person. That is partly why I have used some personal anecdotes, to help us focus on reality.

I've also tried to look at the bigger picture, beyond the shores of Aotearoa New Zealand. How long, for example, can our small planet sustain present tensions and stresses? What will happen if we can't find remedies?

My aim is to encourage you, the reader, to think about what is happening to society around us. Therefore, I've raised many questions, although the answers are not always obvious.

You might have different opinions about some of the ideas expressed. Good. Email me (bryantgw@xtra.co.nz) or contact me on Facebook. I love debate.

Enjoy the read.

George Bryant

---

[1] *Macbeth*, William Shakespeare, Act V Sc 5

PART A

Everyone is unique and has value. We are all searching for happiness but lacking in compassion. We keep wanting more but is there a limit? How do we react to tough times? My cancer scare.

1
More Thinking About Life

Famous scientist Albert Einstein once said, "Thinking is hard work; that's why so few do it."

As a young student I didn't think much. I simply tried to learn, or memorise, whatever was put in front of me.

My first few years at university weren't much different. However, I soon discovered that rote learning had a ceiling. In order to progress, both academically and in life generally, it was vital to think, to analyse, to critique, to actually use one's brain to work things out. It was, indeed, hard work at first but a course in philosophy proved helpful.

Standing in front of a classroom of keen, bright students started a personal thinking revolution. Survival required thinking. Evaluating *Wuthering Heights* or plumbing the depths of Shakespearian tragedies called for considerable thought power.

I soon found myself compiling articles for journals, probing educational concepts. Subsequent involvement in politics and various social institutions led to thinking about the economy and the dynamics of a functioning, rapidly diversifying social scene.

Six decades later I realised I had written and published twenty-five books, and as many booklets. There was so much I wanted to know, so many questions to ask about life and the progress, or otherwise, of society.

I've investigated many social issues and aspects of education, politics and religion. Topics have included euthanasia, abortion, poverty, climate change, political correctness, racism, pain and suffering, and the future. I've compiled biographies and the stories of some major organisations. And I've tried to answer big questions like: Is there life after death? Why do good people do bad things? Are single sex schools better for girls? What enables disabled people to overcome great difficulties? And many more.

More thinking

The title of this book is *More Thinking About Life*. I say 'more' because it's really a sequel to *Life Is...An ordinary Kiwi reflects.*[1] In that book I wrote about the fun, beauty and fragility of life. I probed big questions like why am I here (on Earth), and the meaning of life. I thought about work, war and peace, pain and suffering, spiritual life, life in retirement, big brother, racism, climate change, the future. Two years later I published a whole book about the future: *New Zealand 2050.*[2]

My mind had a rest for a year while I cared for my lovely wife. And then something triggered it into action again.

I began to rethink. Einstein was right. It is often hard work – hard to clarify the boundaries of the issue or problem, hard to find solutions, and hard to challenge people to action.

I continue to think about poverty amidst plenty and the wide gap between the rich and the poor and wonder why we can't spread wealth more evenly. I continue to think about increasing political correctness and the effect it has on our behaviour and what we can or cannot say. I wonder how long we can continue producing, consuming and depleting our natural resources. I worry about the increasing intolerance and violence in our society and the lack of concern for others. I contemplate diminishing aspects of democracy and the growing loneliness and unhappiness of so many citizens.

When one considers the world scene there is much to think about – global poverty and malnutrition, the plight of refugees, international tensions and conflicts, man's inhumanity, the treatment of women, the spreading of disinformation, increasing authoritarianism, the stockpiling of ever more destructive weaponry, cybersecurity, and artificial intelligence.

The world is quite a different place from when I was a child. There was no television then, or internet or cell phones. We didn't even have a fridge, washing machine or vacuum cleaner. There was no KFC or Coke and my father's Ford Prefect could not compare to my new Mazda. Almost everyone went to church or belonged to a club and seemed to care more for each other. The population was not as diverse as it is now.

Times have changed since the middle of last century. Then, the world seemed so stable and ordered. Now, it appears unstable and disordered.

There is so much more to think about.

[1] *Life Is…An Ordinary Kiwi Reflects,* DayStar Books, 2020

[2] *New Zealand 2050,* DayStar Books, 2022

2
We're All Different

I am unique. You are unique. There's no-one else in the world exactly like me or you. Fascinating.

I'm special – but when I look in the mirror each morning, I don't feel I am. My hair's falling out, my eyes are a bit fuzzy, the number of wrinkles is growing, and my mind is cluttered up with things to do. Besides, my wonky knee hurts.

Then, the beautiful tui singing outside my window suddenly reminds me that I am the only person like me in the whole universe, despite my hair, eyes, wrinkles and knee. Wow!

It actually took some years for me to appreciate that each person is different. Oh yes, there are look-a-likes and similar personalities but, essentially, no two people are exactly the same. No two people have the same mix of life experiences, knowledge, emotions, attitudes, world perspectives…We all have distinct identities.

Please don't ask me the scientific or medical reasons for my uniqueness. I'm not trained as a scientist or medical professional. However, I do know that my genetic makeup, my DNA, is only one factor that makes me different from my sister, friend, neighbour and everyone else. And even twins, who have the same DNA, are not absolutely identical.

There are other things as well. I've never seen a body quite like mine! Nor have I seen anyone with a similar combination of talents, skills and interests, although they might well have one or two of them.

Psychologists tell me my personality is unique, too. Although some people might be similarly 'outgoing' in nature they don't have the same blend of experiences, knowledge and behaviour that has moulded me since my birth. The way I perceive the world, the habits I develop, the goals I set and the relationships I form are never exactly the same as anyone else's.

I'm a human being, not a four-legged animal, not a machine, not just a labour unit, or a sexual or economic object, not a pawn in the universe with a preconceived destiny – but a person who thinks, reasons, communicates and has feelings. The biblical psalmist expressed it well, "I praise you (God) because I am fearfully and wonderfully made."[1]

Special

How does it make me feel, to be special?

Well, it's good for my self-esteem. I feel I'm worth something, so I set goals, work hard, form valuable relationships, and enjoy the environment. I find meaning and purpose. If I felt I was a nobody I could be quite depressed.

I don't have to try to be anyone else. Although I gain inspiration from my sports heroes and favourite film stars, I realise I can never be them. I accept myself as I am. In Shakespeare's play, *Hamlet*, Polonius gives his son Laertes some advice as he leaves for university: "To thine own self be true."[2] He wants his son to be true to his principles and who he is, and not try to be someone else.

As a unique human being I can do my own thing, work on my weaknesses, build on my strengths and be free to forge my own path through life. Of course, I live in community and need to adapt to life around me if I want to make progress but, essentially, I am me. I can therefore contribute my unique skills, talents and personality to help others who will, I hope, trust me.

How is difference to be treated?

As special, unique individuals we expect to be treated with respect by those who deal with us – tradesmen and women, professionals, departmental officers, the Government. Politicians need to encompass our uniqueness. We reasonably expect to be treated with dignity, no matter who we are, and have our rights protected. Unfortunately, this is not always the case. We are justly horrified at the treatment some human beings receive both in this country and around the world, be it through bullying, fraud, assaults, rape, or so-called lateral damage in wars...The list is endless.

In my retirement I've enjoyed listening to the life stories of others – so many different and exciting experiences from unique individuals. I often think of the interesting people I've met throughout life – the brilliant teacher who always wore a gown, looking like a bat when he ran; the Afro-Canadian who read his Bible as we crossed Canada by train; the Prime Minister who chatted with me over a ceremonial dinner; the mime artist who stared at me for a good five minutes without moving a muscle; and the tearful little girl holding a teddy bear looking for her mother.

Worth

Yes, life is precious, but how much is it worth?

The internet informs us of multiple attempts to define the cost of a human body, in terms of its various elements. Costs range from a few thousand dollars to $45 million according to the Indiana University School of Medicine, which noted that bone marrow would be $23 million.[3]

A human being is, of course, much more than just a body, although in our materialistic society we tend to see humans as economic units, in monetary terms. Governments and institutions work like this. How much, for example, does it cost to keep a person in good health, to provide various insurances, to protect from injury or death, to provide certain infrastructure, to compensate for wrong imprisonment?

As an economic statistic the price on the head of human beings varies greatly, depending on the state of a country's economy and resources available. Estimates of a statistical life range from US$1 million to US$10 million. In 2019 the New Zealand Transport Authority placed the value of a statistical life at $4.53 million.[4]

Human life is priceless

Human life, however, cannot really be measured in dollars and cents. Any devoted parent will tell you the life of their son or daughter is priceless. You just can't put a dollar amount on them. Human beings are worth far more than dollars and cents. No price can be put on love and kindness, a caring personality, a great sense of humour, or a person's dignity.

Society has progressed, thankfully, from the abominable practices of the slave trade in which people were sold for their labour. But, unfortunately, human trafficking and exploitation still exists in some parts of the world.

Since human life is inherently valuable it needs to be protected at all costs. That's why we have laws against harming and killing people on the one hand, and human rights laws on the other. That's why we need to be careful in passing laws on issues like abortion, euthanasia, and healthcare.

When we fail to respect the sanctity of life, when we fail to administrate for individual uniqueness, society suffers.

"The right to life, I postulate, is the foundation stone of all other human rights. It refers to an inherent, 'supreme' right that reflects the most central values to humankind – self-preservation and dignity."[5]

[1] *The Bible*, Psalm 139:14
[2] *Hamlet*, Act 1 Scene 3
[3] https://medicine.iu.edu
[4] https:/www.wikipedia.org
[5] Louise Arbour, United Nations Commissioner for Human Rights, 9 December, 2005

3
Seeking Happiness

Happiness is the one thing human beings seem to desire more than anything else.

Everyone is looking for it. Everyone wants to be happy, and they will do almost anything to get it. In fact, it becomes an obsession with some people.

Most New Zealanders (76%) say they are happier than much of the rest of the world, according to a world survey.[1] That is not surprising, since we live in a peaceful, well endowed, democratic land, a long way from the world's major trouble spots. Even so, there is much underlying discontent. The same survey shows that over half of the New Zealand population think society is in decline and that the politicians don't care about them.

Many of us think that possessing things will make us happy – plenty of money, a good job, a roof over our heads, a new car, good food, wearing the newest fashions, or acquiring the latest technology. In themselves these might make us a little more comfortable, even if we have to pile up a huge debt to acquire them but, in ourselves, we may feel no happier, especially if we rely on them alone. Wealth isn't the key to true happiness. The world is full of unhappy millionaires.

Or maybe we look for happiness in chasing pleasure – having a good time, an exhilarating para-glide, boozing with the mates, a casual sexual encounter, courting popularity, pursuing idols of one sort or another, binge movie-viewing, popping pills. Relying on circumstances like this, pursuing moments of hyped-up delight, won't help us reach a happy goal.

We may experience passing moments of enjoyment, rapture even, but feel empty and unfulfilled, not really happy after all.

True happiness

True happiness is something different and longer-lasting. It doesn't depend on external factors but on one's inner self – one's attitude to life. Ancient Roman Emperor and philosopher, Marcus Aurelius, summed it up: "Very little is needed to make a happy life; it is all within yourself, in your way of thinking."[2] And ancient Greek philosopher, Aristotle, said "Happiness depends upon ourselves."[3]

Well, their philosophy is basically correct. However, the government of a country also has a part to play. It's difficult to be happy if your air and rivers are polluted or there are not enough green places for children to play or if a struggling economy can't provide you with a job or if the health system makes you wait too long for treatment.

So, what is true happiness? The word 'contentment' sums it up. As the ancient philosophers noted, it's an inner state of being. A happy person is one who is content or satisfied with life, possessing inner peace, and is in accord with others and the surrounding environment.

True happiness is not produced by momentary rushes of adrenalin, such as the view of an awesome sunset or the purchase of a new car or the celebration of a success although these may well contribute to one's general wellbeing.

Saint Paul expressed it so well: "I have learned to be content whatever the circumstances. I know what it is to be in need, and I know what it is to have plenty. I have learned the secret of being content in any and every situation, whether well fed or hungry, whether living in plenty or in want."[4]

We all have our ups and downs in life. That's normal.

The world we live in can easily make us stressed and unhappy. So many bad things happen. Every day the media invades our homes with distress from overseas – wars, poverty, hunger, terror attacks, human trafficking, refugees in flight, gender inequality, corruption.

Our local news is sometimes not much better – violence, smash and grab raids, homicides, broken homes, child abuse, environmental disasters.

We may struggle to make ends meet economically. We may be a victim of violence or sexual abuse. We may have suffered the loss of a loved one or close friend, or we might have health problems or live in continual physical pain. We may have low self-esteem, feel insecure and lonely and have trouble making friends. Life may have dealt with us unfairly.

There are hosts of issues that can make us feel unhappy. As a consequence, we tend to lash out, continually complain, bear grudges, blame and hurt others and develop negative feelings about ourselves and others.

I have come across unhappy people who have suffered abuse as children in one form or another, others who have never really grieved over a loss, and a number who have lived for years in chronic pain.

It's not the aim of this book to probe the reasons for unhappiness. There are many.

However, no matter how discouraged we might be, whatever the reasons, there is a lot of research and advice on how to cure such a state, such as making friends, learning new skills, setting attainable goals, exercising regularly, enjoying nature…Swallowing lots of pills is never a lasting cure.

Contentment requires more than this. Personally, I have tried to practise it over the years. It hasn't been easy at times for, like most of us, I've had some real downs. However, from experience, I pass on to you some of the secrets of finding true happiness, of being content.

Some guides for happiness

(i) Life is worth living. Find meaning.

(ii) Discover and use your talents.

(iii) Develop a career that gives you satisfaction.

(iv) Set worthy goals and achieve them.

(v) Build strong family and friendship ties. Learn to relate well to other people and accept them for who they are.

(vi) Contribute something of worth to society, both through your career and as a community volunteer, working within a team.

(vii) Grow as a person. A happy person is someone who cares for him/herself and attends to personal growth.

(viii) Maintain a positive and balanced outlook.

(ix) Appreciate the beauty of your natural environment.

(x) Exercise regularly, and look after your health.

(xi) Develop the spiritual side of your personality.

Contented people are sociable, unselfish, humble, and show compassion. They tend to have a serenity about them. They are fulfilled and satisfied with life, and treat every day as a blessing, whatever it brings.

For me, the real secret of being content resides in taking time out to reflect on life, pausing amidst the busyness – to ponder who I am, what values I stand for, and what living the human life really means.

Famous civil rights campaigner, Mahatma Gandhi, once claimed that "Happiness is when what you think, what you say, and what you do are in harmony."[5]

[1] Ipsos Global Happiness Survey, 2024 (https://www.ipsos.com/en-nz)
[2] www.setquotes.com
[3] www.pursuit-of-happiness.org
[4] *The Bible*, Philippians 4:11-13
[5] www.socratic-method.com

4
Diminishing Empathy

Have you ever heard comments like these?

"I tried to outline what was wrong with me but she didn't seem to want to know."

"I was deeply hurt by his critical, somewhat judgemental comment. He really didn't understand."

"I spent two weeks in hospital and my best friend never came to see me. However, she did message me a brief note on her phone."

Are we ceasing to care? Is the practice of empathy on the wane? Are social dynamics and the busyness of life forcing us to retreat from understanding the predicaments of others? Are we becoming somewhat detached from people's needs because we are so occupied looking after ourselves?

To the casual observer this may not be apparent. Diminishing empathy is a trait that stealthily creeps up on us, as we try to cope with an increasingly divided, aggressive society.

Empathy is one of the essential aspects that makes us truly human. It is that part of human nature that helps us genuinely connect with other people, and build trust. It enables us to step into their shoes and feel how they feel.

Another word for empathy is 'compassion'. When we are compassionate, we reach out to others and become more inclusive and connected. We appreciate different opinions and cultures. We try to relieve suffering and restore self-worth. Conflicts are more readily resolved, in a peaceful way. Relationships are restored.

However, when empathy is lacking, and people are concerned only for themselves, the consequences are negative. Personal ego and selfishness dictate what we do or don't do. People attack people. They are numbed to the inhumane horrors we witness daily in the media. Oppression, crime and inequality results. Lack of empathy leads to conflict and war.

A personal note

I've always been someone who enjoys meeting people – chatting, sharing, learning. My wife has always said I am 'gregarious'. However, I've recently noticed that certain socio-political trends are leading me to retreat a little, to think more carefully about how involved I become. The need to be politically correct, curbs on the freedom to speak my mind, fear of being unfairly labelled by radical elements in society, and technological gadgetry – all constrain me to think twice about who to relate to and how.

While driving to a golf game I was talking about something important to my mate in the passenger seat. He wasn't responding. I looked over and saw him absorbed with his cell phone. Frustrating.

I went to see a bank official but was directed to a machine set in the wall, but I needed help to make it work.

I phoned for an interview with my insurance agent but was told to select from a number of Frequently Answered Questions. The answer to my problem wasn't there. I sent an email embedded in their website only to receive a stock, irrelevant reply. I'm still trying!

The supermarket queue was very long so I was directed to do the check-out myself; a learning process, I guess.

My doctor was too busy. There was a three-week wait, or I could have a telephone discussion. The nurse saw me, took a picture of the lump on my back and sent it to him. Later that day I received an antibiotic prescription via email.

Something is happening in the world around us. We're gradually being disconnected. Face-to-face conversations and person-to-person relationships, are becoming a scarce commodity. The machine is taking over. It's all becoming artificial and impersonal. Is it no wonder that such impersonal detachment is resulting in burgeoning loneliness and diminishing empathy. Business slogans like 'We Care' don't impress any more.

It never used to be like this. Of course, there are many individuals and groups who do care. Compassion is still around.

Some people are working hard to counteract varied human trauma caused by modern living, doing their best to empathise, although it is sometimes a challenge to love the unlovely.

Nevertheless, contact with the world outside the front door is shrinking. We spend too much time hiding behind screens, little boxes that capture our attention, leaving scarcely any spare time to play or party with neighbours.

There are 5.03 million internet users in Aotearoa New Zealand, 95.7% of the population, and 6.84 million mobile phones – 130.3% of the population.[1] And 81.4% of Kiwis are active social media users, spending an average of two hours and 15 minutes every day on various networks.[2]

I find these figures staggering, although unsurprising. No doubt there are benefits from all this electronic usage. We can keep in touch; for example, with family and friends quickly and over long distances. We can learn lots of new information, especially now that artificial intelligence has infiltrated the social scene. We can shop from home, provide efficiencies in business and gauge the distance from the golf flag.

However, there's a downside, of which psychologists and sociologists readily inform us. They tell us face-to-face communication skills are taking a slide. We are losing the art of conversation. Interactions between couples and families are being disrupted. It's called 'society disconnect' due to 'technoference'.

The Australian Government has just banned social media platforms for under-16-year-olds, because they are affecting mental health and sleep habits, and distracting young people from 'more important' activities. Will New Zealand follow suit?

Much research has been done about this. One survey showed that higher levels of technology use mean less time spent together, less satisfaction and connection with each other and higher levels of depression and anxiety.[3] New Zealand teenagers spend 42 hours a week online, well above the OECD average of 35 hours. That's six hours a day! Staggering.[4] Unfortunately, online activity also promotes cyberbullying and false information.

Recently, the New Zealand Herald reported comments from educational psychologist, Kathryn Burkett. She said screen time was destroying children's ability to concentrate, so much so that they are displaying ADHD (Attention Deficiency Hyperactivity Disorder) behaviour. Classroom teachers are having to use approaches that 'quieten things down'.[5]

So, the New Zealand Government, in line with other countries, has now banned cell phones from the nation's classrooms. They note the distractions they have caused, leading to lower student achievement. One survey showed that 35% of teens admit to using smartphones to cheat during tests.[6]

It is believed that the absence of phones will lead to more positive outcomes. Various surveys have found that children in schools where cell phones have been banned do better.

The constant hiding behind screens leads to a focus on self and narcissism. Avid social media users, both children and adults, become unaware of what's going on around them.

Consequently, they lose the ability to express themselves and fail to grow as people. They become unempathetic.

Hope?

Thank goodness I have empathetic friends, people who care, who cheer me up when I need it, people who understand, and tolerate my inadequacies.

The restoration of face-to-face communication is urgent. It is essential we combat the bad effects of rising digital technology use. We need to re-learn the art of looking a person in the eye and reaching out. Human connection is vital for mental health, commitment and intimacy.

Humanitarian and Nobel Prize winner, Albert Schweitzer, once said, "The purpose of human life is to serve and show compassion and the will to help others."[7]

The world definitely needs more empathy.

[1] httpx://dataportal.com
[2] socialmedia.org, 2023
[3] David Schramm, Professor at Utah State University, 2019
[4] Report from OECD Programme for International Student Assessment, May 2021
[5] *New Zealand Herald*, 6 August, 2024
[6] www.commonsensemedia.org (Benenson Strategy Group)
[7] https://socratic-method.com

5
We Always Want More

"More! More!"

This word was often heard at our dinner table when our daughter was very young. She was often not satisfied with the amount she had just eaten and wanted more.

We're no different. As individuals, societies and nations we all keep wanting more. We never seem to be satisfied with what we have – more food, more clothes, more electronic gadgets, smart-phones and televisions (one in every room), new cars, better lifestyles, improved household appliances…anything to make life more comfortable and exciting.

Wanting more seems to be a natural human desire. We're never satisfied with what we have and want to keep moving forward, always inventing and producing new things, forever producing and consuming. Some call it 'progress'. Others call it 'greed'.

We all want progress. We have a fixation on growth. Politicians and economists are happy when the Gross Domestic Product (GDP) shows strong increases, and depressed when it doesn't. We wait in anticipation as the Reserve Bank deliberates on whether to raise or lower the Official Cash Rate (OCR) because its decision could make or break us. We strive for whatever is bigger and better. Progress means increased sales, greater profit, bigger dividends and more wealth. Lagging behind Australia and the rest of the western world is not an option.

The assumption is that greater and greater production ushers in prosperity, with more benefits for everyone, but it doesn't work that way. Poverty keeps expanding as the gap between rich and the poor widens, proving that Scottish economist Adam Smith's trickle-down theory just doesn't work. It's the same all over the world, especially in Western nations. The richest 10% own 76% of the world's wealth, according to the World Inequality Report, 2024.[1] In our own country it's much the same: the poorest half of adults, 1.8 million, have only 2% of all wealth.[2]

The 'produce or perish' philosophy simply produces inequality. "The story of perpetually growing consumption for all has turned out to be a fairy tale."[3]

People want not only material progress but social progress as well – improved health facilities, more housing, a solution to increasing crime, improved education…The list is long.

A brief glimpse into the past will show we have indeed progressed in leaps and bounds on many fronts, albeit at considerable cost to the environment. General total wellbeing has surpassed what it used to be.

And now we have started experimenting with artificial intelligence and robots galore, something thought of only in the realms of fantasy a few years ago.

However, the basic fact remains. If we don't produce enough to satisfy our individual and collective wants, we heavily criticise the Government and suffer social, psychological and workplace trauma. We become dissatisfied, and flee to Australia or somewhere else where the grass appears greener.

I'm not an economist. Far from it. I'm just an ordinary Kiwi who tries to make sense of what's going on around him.

Sustainability?

Nevertheless, I'm thinking that sooner or later our madcap desire to produce and consume will not only deplete our non-renewable resources of oil, coal and gas but even make it difficult for renewable resources – water, geothermal power and wind – to cope. Our demands for more will outstrip available resources.

So, my question is: For how long will we be able to sustain our production/consumption cycle as the population keeps growing and resources dwindle? Our economic growth depends on energy but we're running out of it. Natural gas, for example, will be depleted in less than ten years. Coal use for electricity will be phased out within the next fifteen years, to reduce carbon emissions.

We'll be relying more and more on renewable resources – providing the rivers keep flowing, the wind keeps blowing and the sun keeps shining.

As I write this there has been a massive spike in electricity prices because of greatly reduced hydro lakes storage, low wind generation and low gas output. Several large businesses have had to close. There may need to be huge imports of Indonesian coal and liquid natural gas.

Unfortunately, we tend to think only short-term, patching up present needs as the population keeps growing. A telling comment was made by the narrator of the movie *Vice*, the story of the former Vice-President of the United States, Dick Cheyne: "As the world becomes more and more confusing, we tend to focus on things that are right there in front of us while ignoring the massive forces that actually change and shape our lives."

Politicians are forever occupied with short-term remedies for present problems – dire housing needs, the cost of living, rotting water pipes, traffic jams, solving transport problems, crime, surgery waiting lists and the like. If the population keeps increasing at the present rate we will always be worrying about these things. The essence of politics is pragmatism, pleasing the people. There are now 5½ million people in NZ. In 50 years, there will be nearly seven million, thus creating more pressure on infrastructure and resources.[4]

More valuable, fertile land will be lost on the outskirts of cities. Native vegetation will continue to be converted into pastures and plantations. More renewable resources will be needed. Our present water usage is the second highest in the OECD.

People in countries like New Zealand, where there is a small population and an apparent abundance of natural resources, are mostly unaware of the seriousness of the situation. They are lulled into a false sense of security.

My argument applies equally to the world scene. Fossil fuels won't last forever. It is generally believed that at the present rate of consumption we will exhaust supplies of oil, gas and coal this century. Some scientists estimate they'll be depleted by 2060, having taken millions of years to form. Water is fast becoming a scarce commodity, and the rape of the Amazon and other forests continues apace.

Limits to growth

I'm thinking. We can't keep going on like this. There must be limits to our growth, a finite end to progress. When will we know if we've had enough?

Back in the 1970s we were warned. I read *Limits to Growth* which sold millions of copies.[5] The authors discussed the very things I'm writing about – the interplay of economics, population growth and the use of finite resources. It stated, in effect, that if we kept using resources the way we were everything would come to a halt in one hundred years. They pleaded for a more sustainable lifestyle.

The book was severely criticised. Like human beings, countries are selfish and protective. No-one likes being told they're going in the wrong direction. They have difficulty facing the truth. The predictions of *Limits to Growth* proved to be remarkably accurate. A number of books and reports on a similar theme have been published since. Major world conferences have been held. Some people have been listening but political action is slow.

Is there any hope?

I do my little bit to conserve, recycle and avoid waste. I notice many governments and organisations are placing considerable emphasis on sustainability but I wonder if their efforts are a little too late, simply delaying the inevitable, barely keeping up with ongoing growth?

As the population increases so does demand. The numbers of people living on this planet are growing rapidly. In the year 1800, 224 years ago, there were only 1.6 billion people on Earth. Now there are over eight billion and the United Nations predicts there will be nearly ten billion by 2050.

How can Earth's resources support so many people? What are the consequences if we can't? The World

Bank already reports that one-quarter of the world's population live below the societal poverty line today, lacking the basic necessities of life such as adequate food and safe drinking water, and decent housing, education and health facilities.[6]

In fact, the United Nations Environment Programme says, "The majority of studies estimate the Earth's capacity is at or beneath eight billion people."[7]

We've already reached our limit!

We are staring in the face of scarcities of basic commodities, economic and environmental disaster and increasing conflicts.

What now?

How do we turn things around? A major universal rethink is urgent. A massive, global effort is required. The planet itself will survive but will the people who inhabit it?

Always an optimist, albeit a realist, I have hope in human ingenuity, and I hope the right sort of leadership will arise, with long-term vision and the will to act.

A revival agenda must include:

- A halt to the nationalistic, selfish belief that nations can survive by themselves. We have only one planet. It is under stress. Co-operative, bold, international solutions are required.

- A change in human behaviour – from wanting more and more, and being satisfied with less. More doesn't necessarily lead to happiness.
- A redistribution of what we have, to iron out inequalities
- A relook at sustainability efforts. How do we convince major polluters to immediately reduce carbon levels?
- Accelerating the introduction and use of renewable resources
- A reconciliation of humans with nature and a halt to deforestation
- A reduction of population growth

The famous French oceanographer, Jacques Cousteau, once said, "Overconsumption and overpopulation underlie every environmental problem we have today."[8]

1   World Inequality Database, https://wid.com
2   Household Net Worth Survey, 2021, www.stats.govt.nz
3   Maja Gopel, *Rethinking Our World*, Scribe, 2023
4   https://stats.govt.nz
5   DH Meadows, DL Meadows, J Randers, WW Behrens, Universe Books, 1972
6   World Economic Forum www.weforum.org

[7] Global Environmental Alert Service/One Planet. How many people? Quoted in article by Martin Kueber in Nature and Environment, Nov 15, 2022

[8] www.azquotes.com

6

When the Going Gets Tough

It's tough when a bright, vivacious 29-year-old is diagnosed with terminal cancer. It's tough when an eight-year-old boy becomes an orphan after his parents and siblings were killed in an horrific accident. It's tough when a spouse has to move into permanent residential care after wonderful decades of married years.

Life is no respecter of persons. Everyone experiences tough times. It's part of life. That's the reality. Suffering is the great leveller. It affects rich and poor, beautiful and ugly, black, brown and white, intelligent and not-so-intelligent.

Twelve per cent of New Zealanders experience ongoing poor or fair health.[1] And 54% of beneficiaries have a health condition or disability.[2]

Our tough time may not be poor health or an accident. We may be struggling to make ends meet financially, a victim of crime, suffering from an unbearable family conflict or a traumatic loss, or going through a housing crisis.

Whatever our tough time it's helpful to realise we don't suffer alone. There are many others who hurt, some worse than us. And it's not always our own fault. It could be an hereditary disease, a chronic illness, an accident or abuse by others.

How do we react?

However, the key is how we react to what befalls us and whether or not we learn anything from the experience. How we react determines how we continue to live.

I've always been in awe of people who manage to cope well with the tough stuff life brings them. I observe, listen, watch and learn, and often wonder how they manage life with a smile and move on. What motivates them?

In 2010 I investigated this. I interviewed 50 ordinary Kiwis who had various major health issues – cerebral palsy, cancer, blindness, spina bifida, paralysis – and other trauma, such as domestic violence, and physical and sexual abuse. I then wrote and published a book titled *Trial to Triumph: Inspiring Stories of Overcomers.* It was almost a best seller!

The first chapter of this book examined 'the undaunted human spirit' and probed the question of why human beings who suffer great trauma pick themselves up, overcome their difficulties and make a success of life: "We can wallow in self-pity, suffer in abject silence or rail against the unseen forces that have determined our fate. We can moan and complain about how unjust the world is. Or, with an undaunted spirit, we can work through our suffering, make the best of it, learn from it and move forward. We can find creative opportunities within our misfortunes."[3]

Since I wrote that I've had to apply 'overcoming' principles to a few of my own life traumas. They work. The eight principles I uncovered still apply.

(i) Accept the situation – and realise what other abilities or talents you might have which you can build on. You don't have to be a victim.

(ii) Have faith in yourself. For example, a woman with no legs started sailing yachts, and a man who was paralysed from the waist down did sky jumps and drove up and down three small mountains in a day to raise funds for charity.

(iii) Develop the right attitude. That is, always be positive, and grateful. The tough time we go through may not be as bad as what other people suffer.

(iv) Set new achievable goals.

(v) Live in hope that things will get better and embrace a wider view of life than your own predicament. Our pain may not be as bad as we think.

(vi) Accept gracefully any support that is offered by caring friends or others.

(vii) Persevere. Never give up. A top Olympic skier

was paralysed after a bad accident and told she would never walk again. Later, she gained her commercial pilot's licence and flew jets and helicopters! She wrote a book *Never Tell Me Never.*[4]

(viii) Cultivate the spiritual. Appreciate things of worth around you and build upon your values.

The whole point is that when the going gets tough we DON'T give up and walk away, become a self-pitying recluse or take to drink or drugs. That approach achieves nothing.

Overcomers 'hang in there' and try to work through their trauma. They don't just survive but move on, enjoying half-a-day at a time, providing inspiration for the rest of us.

There's always hope. Tough times usually don't last forever, for life does have its better moments.

---

[1] New Zealand Health Survey, Ministry of Health www.health.govt.nz

[2] www.weag.govt.nz

[3] Page 26, *Trial to Triumph*, DayStar Books, 2010

[4] Shepherd, Janine, *Never Tell Me Never*, Random House, 2007

7
Living With Cancer

Almost half of New Zealanders are behind in general health checks, according to a 2024 survey.[1]

More than half of us only visit a doctor when we have to.[2]

Thirty per cent of men 40 years of age and over are behind on prostate screening.[3]

Many Kiwis don't look after their health very well. There are some valid reasons for this, especially the cost of visiting a doctor or specialist, waiting times and accessibility. Add to these an element of fear that the doctor may find something wrong.

With males there still exists a traditional attitude of 'she'll be right'. My father was like that. He actually prided himself for never going to a doctor. Unfortunately, he died of lung cancer when he was relatively young. Maybe it could have been prevented.

In this day and age regular medical check-ups can possibly prevent an illness or disease from happening or worsening. It's important to watch self-care and be proactive.

Personally, I have been through some frightening health moments, the worst being a blood clot on my left lung and prostate cancer.

My cancer story

Like most of us I dreaded the 'big C' and never thought it would happen to me.

Every year 3000 Kiwi men are found to have prostate cancer, and 600 die from it. And many of those who die from something else are found to have had cancer of the prostate as well!

When I was middle-aged my doctor started giving me regular prostate checks. Over time the PSA (Prostate-Specific Antigen) started to rise. When it reached 19.49 the doctor didn't seem unduly worried because the prostate was not enlarged. Indeed, he assured me a rising level didn't necessarily indicate cancer. I should only worry if it jumped to 60 or 70 or more!

I had heard that guys who reached that level were simply given hormone treatment and sent home to eek out their remaining years. I didn't want that.

My GP (General Practitioner) did suggest hormone injections if I was worried. These would suppress the testosterone and reduce the PSA level, but not cure the cancer.

However, I confess I was becoming a little agitated. Naturally, I had checked with other men all of whom had much lower PSA levels, and I found they had all had some sort of remedial treatment.

Proactive

It was time to be proactive. So, I asked my GP to refer me to a specialist (specialist Number 1). We are fortunate in my city to have some of the world's key cancer specialists.

The meeting took place seven days later. He was quick to tell me that he wouldn't operate "because of my age", but he did take a biopsy the very next day, without anaesthetic but with painkillers. This consisted of a number of large needles being inserted through my rectum. It was uncomfortable but there was no pain.

At the follow-up appointment he simply announced, "You've got cancer." An MRI[4] scan was ordered. It was a nervous four-month wait. I had never had an MRI and suffered a little from claustrophobia. My nervousness meant the scan took longer than usual because I kept moving.

But it confirmed the cancer, although it was low grade and slow growing. "Nothing to worry about," I was told, "but we need to keep an eye on it." Needless to say, I was a somewhat relieved.

Even though I had contracted low-grade cancer my amateurish medical sense told me that cancer has a habit of growing, and I wanted to do something about it.

"What happens now?" I asked.

Active surveillance

"We'll put you on active surveillance for a year."

This simply meant a blood test mid-year and another MRI at the end of it – not very 'active' really.

The specialist did mention a procedure – brachytherapy – but I had read about this and didn't like the idea. It sounded rather messy and involved two general anaesthetics. In retrospect I wish I had taken up this suggestion; it may have saved a lot of discomfort later. But I wasn't to know what the future held. I opted for a year's active surveillance instead.

However, because I was anxious, I organised extra blood tests. The PSA level dropped by a few points. Were things turning the corner or was it a false hope? No. It leapt up again to 22.37. I was in trouble.

It wasn't surprising, therefore, to find that the second MRI scan showed an increase of the cancer with some of it very aggressive. The specialist then ordered another biopsy (perineal) under anaesthetic, in order to pinpoint its density and location with greater accuracy. By February 2017 the PSA level had reached 24.02.

At the age of 78 I didn't wish to die. There were still too many things to do and enjoy.

The medical professionals kept telling me that "at my age" I would sooner or later die of something (true) and "it might be prostate cancer." But I kept thinking, why should I die of prostate cancer when there are so many world experts here in Tauranga?

The clear implication was that if I had prostate cancer I might well live for a few more years anyway, especially if I undertook hormone therapy – so there was no need to worry too much. Yeah, right!

I'm sure these medical people were all well-meaning but inwardly I rebelled at this sort of philosophy, and wasn't prepared to accept the fact that, if I had cancer, I could do little about getting rid of it, "because of my age."

I had come across many men in their 80s and 90s who were still making a great contribution to society.

And what about my health anyway? Does it really matter how old someone is? Surely one's health should be the key factor.

While I freely admit there might be some risks with certain medical procedures the older you get, if one's health is the prime consideration (not age) then surely safe ways and means can be found – in this day and age with 'all these experts around'.

Initial shock

When I did discover I had cancer it was a bit of a shock, because I had none of the usual symptoms. I wasn't urinating frequently and had no loss of blood, no pain or burning sensation and no lower back pain or pain in my pelvic area. The cancer had quietly crept up on me.

In the past I've always actively pursued solutions to my problems, without procrastinating, so I immediately began to do something about this one.

The whole thing was now becoming somewhat scary and serious. What was I to do?

The specialist must have sensed my unease so I agreed to have a full body scan (Gallium PSMA) at Auckland's Mercy Hospital – an unpleasant 90-minute procedure during which I became somewhat radioactive. It was excruciatingly painful trying to urinate but being unable to do so. Afterwards, I was told to keep clear of pregnant mothers and little children for several hours.

The scan result was reassuring, for it showed no cancer in the rest of my body, the disease being confined to the prostate gland itself.

"What happens now?" I asked again. The specialist said he would give me hormone injections.

"Not satisfactory," I thought. I later discovered that if one kept having hormone injections over a period of years there were negative side effects, including the loss of cognitive ability. And I didn't want that.

Something had to be done, and if hormone injections weren't the answer, what was?

I re-read the material about brachytherapy. This seemed

to be the only viable treatment for my age and situation, so I asked the specialist if he would refer me to his colleague whom I knew carried out this procedure (specialist Number 2). He told me I would have to argue a case, because of some high-grade cancer, a high PSA level and "my age".

I must confess I started becoming a little irritated at this frequent reference to my age. What about my health?

So, I wrote a letter to specialist Number 2 and "'argued my case.'" By this time, I had had five diagnostic procedures. I told him that while I didn't know all the details, I was fully aware I had prostate cancer, that it was growing and some of it was aggressive. My only option, I told him, was to have hormone treatment, with its unwanted side effects. Would he please explore the possibility of brachytherapy. I had no heart disease, diabetes, multiple sclerosis, motor neurone or life-threatening diseases – but I had prostate cancer. I also mentioned that if there was no intervention the cancer would spread to other parts of my body, although the PET/CT[5] scan showed it was clear at the moment.

He agreed to see me.

When I stepped inside the door, he commended me on the "excellent" letter. I sat there for some minutes while he perused all the diagnostic detail to date.

Then he turned to me and asked, "Do you want to be cured?"

"Of course," I said.

"Well, I will recommend you to my colleague (specialist Number 3) for high dosage radiation (HDR). But first, hop in there," he said, pointing to the bed in the surgery next door.

A nurse appeared, with a long needle, and injected me under the ribs with a hormone capsule. I received these regularly until the procedure took place and had them for eighteen months afterwards.

The hormone, Zoladex, depresses testosterone, decreases sex drive, produces numerous hot flushes, swollen breasts, shrinking testicles and increased my weight by several kilos.

Brachytherapy

After an anxious three-month wait I met the third specialist, who spent some time determining whether I was a suitable candidate. I must have been, because she decided to proceed with high dosage brachytherapy.

Thus began a hectic, and somewhat harrowing, nine months which included a urine flow test, three CAT scans, a thirty-minute examination by an anaesthetist, an electrocardiogram to see if my heart could cope, and then brachytherapy on 22 August 2017. One of the scans was to check the structure of my pelvic area so the needles they were going to insert would not be impeded.

Fifteen needles were to be inserted into my prostate and iridium 192 would be sent into it via these needles, with different dosage strengths directed to the various cancer areas.

While I didn't meet one of the requirements for this procedure (Some of my cancer grades were too high.), I was determined to proceed anyway.

Seven days beforehand I was on a strict low fibre diet. A spinal anaesthetic rendered me unconscious, although I was given the option of staying awake and watching it all, an option I politely refused.

I also opted to be a guinea pig for a new strategy to help protect the rectum from radiation. This was a Space Oar hydrogel, inserted between the prostate and the rectum. It would dissolve after a couple of months. My feet were put in stirrups and fifteen needles inserted through the perineum. A catheter was also inserted.

While I was semi-conscious a CAT scan was taken to check that the needles were in the right position. I then spent two hours awake, but numb below the waist (a peculiar sensation of paralysis) while the team decided the amount of radiation to be put through the various needles.

I was wheeled back into theatre. Three nurses appeared each holding some long tubes which they proceeded to screw on to the ends of the needles, and I was then zapped with various dosages, accompanied by different buzzing sounds, for thirty-five minutes. There was no implant of iodine seeds, as some men have had. At the completion the needles were suddenly removed.

All this was followed by fifteen days of external radiation. Two weeks after radiation the effects hit me, lasting for two months, two of the worst months in my life!

I suffered severe fatigue and total exhaustion at times, having lots of sleeps, sometimes three times a day. I had little energy or strength. It was hard to concentrate.

I soon learnt to go with the flow and pace myself – very difficult for an active person! There were urinating problems – six times a night – although I had a pill to counter the discomfort – and irregular and uncomfortable bowel issues. As 2018 began I had climbed back almost to normal.

Three and a half months after brachytherapy my PSA level decreased to 0.02 – "the best it can get," said the nurse – and has been like that for the past seven years. I was cured!

Learnings

My trial with cancer has taught me a number of things.

1. Have regular medical checks.
2. Be proactive. If your PSA level is rising and your prostate is enlarging, even a little, do something about it. Tell your GP you want to see a specialist, and work with the specialist for appropriate treatment.
3. Be willing to undergo at least nine months of tests, procedures and discomfort – if you want to be cured.
4. Diligently read all the brochures and pamphlets about how, for example, to prepare for CAT scanning, how to prepare bowel and bladder, dietary guides, managing fatigue, and how to use an enema effectively.
5. Trust in the expertise of the oncology medical team.
6. It is important to keep a healthy prostate by eating a balanced diet. There is a lot of advice on the internet.

    (i) plenty of fruit and vegetables

    (ii) selenium – Brazil nuts, wheat germ, herring and other seafood, eggs, sunflower seeds, cashews and garlic

(iii) anti-oxidants – processed tomatoes (spaghetti, sauce, sun-dried) juice, broccoli, green tea, beans, and peanuts

(iv) healthy fats – olive oil, nuts, and avocados

(v) limited consumption of red meat and more fish

(vi) regular exercise

I have the highest of praise for the professionalism and skill of the Bay of Plenty oncology team. They do a tremendous job.

I want to thank my caring wife, Joan, who accompanied me to interviews, helped me with various treatments, coped so well with the effects of my radiation, and prayed for me.

My trial with cancer, from when it was first verified, lasted two years and five months.

I'm most grateful I've been acquitted.

---

[1] Survey reported in *NZ Doctor*, 8.3.24

[2] Tend Health Index. Reported in Newshub 2.7.23

[3] Ibid

[4] Magnetic Resonance Imaging

[5] Position Emission Tomography and Computed Tomography

PART B

Words matter, but how free are we
to say what we want to say? What
happened to truth? We need wiser leaders,
a greater awareness of people's spirituality,
and more clarity about the Treaty of Waitangi.
Is the end of human civilisation in sight?
What hope is there?

8
Words Matter

I cringe when I hear the violent and often hate-filled rhetoric of American politicians. Nothing seems off limits.

I react negatively to the overuse of swear words in television comedies.

I get annoyed when people I don't know begin a phone conversation with "How are you?" I'm sure they don't have the faintest interest in my wellbeing.

I become a little frustrated when a sales-person asks me if there is "anything else," when I've spent a lot of time searching and finding exactly what I want. And after I've paid for what I found they tell me to "Have a good one," whatever that means.

Nevertheless, like most people, I enjoy expressions of love or concern or the occasional compliment.

Words are vital for communication and social progress, even though they are often over-used or misused. They make the world go round.

They fly at us from various directions every day – the television, newspapers, text messages, advertisements, computers, people. They guide us, inform us, and help us connect with others and the world around us. They enable us to perceive reality and open our minds to truth.

They affect us, negatively or positively, from great distances and throughout time. For example, many emotions have been stirred by Shakespeare's use of words or by a birthday card from another country with the signature phrase 'I love you'. Without words, human beings would revert to being grunting stone-agers.

Words not only reflect what we think but also tell us what to think. They so readily reveal character. They convey our thoughts and feelings. When we open our mouths, we let people know what sort of person we are, for what comes out of the mouth comes from the heart. Our words give us away.

"Words have the power to make things happen," said theologian Frederick Buechner.[1] They can carry tremendous weight.

Blessing or curse

Words can be a blessing or a curse. They can build someone up or tear them down, hurt or encourage, praise or condemn, and promote or destroy reputations.

Bullying via text messaging has led people to suicide. Communities and nations have been destroyed by dictators using hate words and propaganda.

The personal slanging matches we read and heard about in the recent United States' election illustrated the worst uses of language. The pronouncement of policies became eclipsed by a barrage of hyperbole and disinformation. One candidate was labelled the 'Anti-Christ' and 'the devil'. Since then, the Prime Minister of Britain has been called 'evil'.

A former New Zealand Minister of Finance recently bewailed the descent into "bile-spewing" and "vitriol" in politics. He pleaded for "normal people" to be more involved or "radical agendas are likely to prevail."[2]

In the New Zealand parliament one party accused its opponents of wanting to 'eliminate' the indigenous people. Such words are emotionally overloaded and so blatantly false. They can cause nothing but harm.

Science tells us words have a direct effect on the brain. Hurtful words can increase the pulse rate or raise blood pressure and ongoing verbal abuse can even cause physical damage through stress.[3]

On the other hand, communities have been revitalised by saints. Freedom of expression has developed healthy communities. Martin Luther's words launched the Reformation. Martin Luther King's words generated racial equality in America. Winston Churchill's words inspired victory in World War 2. And Mother Teresa's words brought hope to the poor of Calcutta.

A whole chapter of the Bible is devoted to the power

of words and the caution to control our tongues, for big things can come from a tiny tongue, just like a small spark can set a forest ablaze.[4]

About 30 years ago a person I thought was my friend came to see me. I hadn't seen him for 30 years. He proceeded to recount all the things he disliked about my beliefs or behaviour and then disappeared. Needless to say, I was momentarily speechless and somewhat dumbfounded. His words have surfaced in my mind regularly since then. I've had considerable trouble erasing them.

Why did he do that? Why do people you have trusted go to such lengths?

Maybe he disagreed with my views more strongly than I had anticipated. Maybe it was a power thing – wanting to put me in my place for not being up to his own standards. It's obvious his words were meant to end any relationship we might have had.

Today

We are facing an era of word control that's stifling free speech, endeavouring to force us to be politically correct, to fit into pre-conceived patterns of behaviour. Vigilance is needed to ensure our language is not weakened or softened. Otherwise, truth will suffer.

I feel unfairly controlled when told I can't use certain words, like 'lazy' or 'stupid' or 'fat' or 'gay', not that I have a need to use them but I used to enjoy freedom to do so. With other words I have to be extra careful. If I want to use the word 'homosexual' or the phrase 'marriage is between male and female' or express anything about a 'trans' person, especially 'preferred pronouns' or talk about 'old' people instead of 'seniors', I might be called to account, even prosecuted.

I'm continually warned that I need to be inclusive in my language in a diverse society. Fair enough. It's important to use words that don't hurt or harm others. But, then, we never know how people will react to what we write or say. Their prejudices erect walls against certain expressions.

A few tips

As a public speaker, author, publisher and teacher of English I've done business with thousands upon thousands of words. Here are a few tips.

1. Think before you speak, or write. Once words have been released, they're difficult to retract, just like trying to squeeze toothpaste back into the tube.

2. Be careful not to use words lazily. They can hurt people without your realising it. When writing, I frequently use a thesaurus to select appropriate words.

Someone once said: "The tongue has no bones but is strong enough to break a heart. So be careful with your words."[5]

3. Be truthful. Avoid gossiping, which can cause much damage. "Let your word 'yes' be 'yes' and your 'no' be 'no'. In other words, say exactly what you mean. Speak truthfully.[6]

4. Use words that build people up. Build bridges with communities. Zig Ziglar, author, salesman and motivational speaker, said: "He climbs highest who helps another up."[7]

5. Encourage. Be positive. Kind words have healing power.

6. Affirm the gifts and talents of others. Compliment. Praise.

7. Don't dwell on certain topics, such as, your bad health, your family feuds, or your past/present problems. Your listeners might get upset.

8. Try and keep abreast of all the new social media words, such as 'viral', 'hashtag', 'blog', 'meme', 'non-binary'.

9. Learning another language helps communication and cultural understanding.

A knowledge of French helps me communicate with my family in southern France. Two courses in Māori language have given me a more in-depth understanding of New Zealand's indigenous culture. Although I never learnt Japanese, I have visited the country three times and picked up phrases which I have since used effectively.

Sigmund Freud once noted the magical power of words: "They can either bring the greatest happiness or the deepest despair."[8]

Our choice of words does matter.

[1] www.quotefancy.com
[2] Steven Joyce, Opinion piece in New Zealand Herald, 11 January, 2025
[3] Article by Christopher Hazell in *PLNU Viewpoint* magazine, July 22, 2017
[4] James 3
[5] Anonymous
[6] James 5:12
[7] www.my.wealthyaffiliate.com
[8] www.verywellmind.com

9
How Free Is Speech?

Are we able to express our opinions freely, without fear of censorship or retaliation?

The ability to do so is being progressively restricted. Our politically correct society is gradually stifling personal opinion and debate. Certain traditional topics and viewpoints are now off limits.

I was raised to believe that freedom of expression was a vital principle of democracy, its lifeblood. If people and groups were allowed to promote their views freely it would lead to better understanding of diverse viewpoints and greater tolerance. I was taught to debate issues robustly both as a speaker and writer. Sadly, that freedom is rapidly waning, in democracies as well as autocracies.

We have become increasingly intolerant of what other people think, especially if it's contrary to what we think. We protest. We drive them off the stage. We censor what they want to say. We counter their ideas with misinformation. We cancel their meetings.

Personally, I confess I often have second thoughts about expressing opinions on a number of topics for fear of being publicly shamed or labelled a racist, sexist, homophobe, Islamaphobe, or something else. My true thoughts on some topics don't see the light of day, for fear of complaints to the police. For example, it's difficult, now, to promote the nuclear family as the foundation for a heathy society or to advance the view that marriage should be between a man and a woman or to ask someone about their cultural background – where they come from or where they were born.

Once I tried to debate a particular issue with a colleague in the foyer of a conference hall. We held opposing views. We had scarcely probed the question when we were shut down by another colleague, either because she didn't like to hear a debate on the matter or, more likely, because she knew my views and didn't want them aired. On another occasion, while speaking at a public meeting, I was hissed at by a particular group as I tried to offer an alternative viewpoint about a topic to which my listeners obviously objected. They just didn't want to hear. Intolerance.

Public speakers

On a larger, more public platform this is what happened with Posie Parker, an anti-trans activist, in Auckland, on March 2023. I discuss this because it's the sort of incident that is occurring too frequently in our democratic society.

She was forced to leave the stage, escorted by police,

without being allowed to offer a word. Hundreds of people with opposing views made so much noise she couldn't be heard. Not only this. They threw water, juice and eggs at her.

Posie Parker was condemned for possibly using hate speech, but the audience hadn't even heard what she was going to say! The hate lay with the protestors! She had to cancel a trip to this country six months later, worried that she would not be protected by police.

Let me be clear. Personally, I had never heard of Posie Parker or seen anything written by her. There is no way I could possibly judge what she might have said. However, I defend her right to say it, just as I defend the right of people to protest peacefully against what she might have said.

Immigration Minister Michael Wood said he condemned her "inflammatory, vile and incorrect world views."[1] Whose world views? The Minister's? His political party's views? A particular organisation's world views? In any democratic society multiple world views are at play. Who can claim what is right and what is wrong, unless it's a clear break with the law. As far as I am aware there was no law against this woman speaking. What was at play here was some sort of moral code.

While Posie Parker wasn't allowed to utter a word, many inflammatory words were uttered about her from protesters and lawyers alleging what she was likely to say. Was her forthcoming speech likely to be a threat to public order, as her critics had alleged? Only if the protesters refused to listen or behave themselves!

At the time the Free Speech Union said public order or safety was not seriously threatened by the public being able to listen to views that the applicants did not agree with. "There's no person or group right not to be offended or hurt by the views of another; hurt in the mind not the body obviously."[2]

It was interesting to note that the High Court rejected a challenge to have her banned from entering the country and speaking.

No matter how controversial a speaker might be it is vital to hear all points of view in a democracy. How else are we to fight disinformation and get to the truth of a matter?

A Curia Market Research poll in September, 2023 found that 75% of the population agreed free speech is an important Kiwi value and 51% believed free speech was under threat.

Cancel culture

What I've just described is an example of 'cancel culture'.

This is a term that has arisen in recent decades to describe what is really a stronger form of old-fashioned censorship. We no longer simply black out sentences from a person's speech. We black out the speaker as well. We cancel the very right to speak.

If we don't like what someone stands for, the ideas they are expressing, then we want nothing to do with them. Anti free-speech people think they know better what we should hear or be allowed to say.

And cancel culture doesn't just apply to speakers. Books and music are banned, products are boycotted and people are fired from their jobs, just because someone or some organisation or some employer finds their views unacceptable. They are silenced. Cancelled.

The classic case of cancel culture occurred over former USA president Donald Trump's support of the 6 January attack on the capitol. He was cancelled out of Twitter and Facebook. Congresswoman Liz Cheney was cancelled and stripped of her position in the Republican Party leadership because she criticised former President Trump's role in the 6 January riots.

Author J.K. Rowling was cancelled for remarks about transgender people. Ellen DeGeneres' show was cancelled when she declared she was lesbian. Outspoken actress and activist Jane Fonda was cancelled from television appearances.

Dr Don Brash, former Leader of New Zealand's National Party and Reserve Bank Governor, was cancelled. Because he opposed Māori favouritism and the abolition of Māori Council Wards his proposed speech to Massey University students was cancelled by the University authorities. The Vice-Chancellor was quoted as saying she "supported free speech on campus but totally opposed hate speech."[3] Surely this was a pre-emptive judgement, based purely on what she thought Brash believed and how his audience might react. How did she know it would be hate speech? A number of public figures criticised the decision on the basis that, whatever his views, he had the right to speak, which he was allowed to do two months later, without any protests. In fact, the question of academic freedom has been an issue in several universities in recent years.

The Peace Action Group tried to prevent renowned world psychologist, Dr Jordan Peterson, from speaking in New Zealand, because of his prior criticism of gender culture and the use or mis-use of preferred pronouns. They were unsuccessful, for Peterson promoted his book *12 Rules for Life* to full houses in our three major cities. However, his Twitter account was cancelled after posting a tweet about misgendering. And Cambridge University revoked an invitation to him as a visiting fellow because, they claimed, he was not inclusive.

Christian evangelist Julian Batchelor led a 'stop co-government' campaign in 2023. He believed moves towards co-government with Māori were undemocratic and racially divisive. A number of venue owners cancelled his reservations in many locations across the country. He criticised them for taking away his right to free speech. One mayor even said Batchelor was not welcome in his area.

Cancel culture annihilates free speech. It doesn't matter whether it's practised by the political left or political right. My examples involve both. The great irony is that the groups that want to stop others speaking freely, because they disagree with their views, expect the same freedom to be granted to themselves.

Hate speech

Fortunately, the New Zealand Government's proposed hate speech laws have been abandoned.

They had been promoted by the 'woke' left and by the Labour Government in response to the 2019 terror attacks on Christchurch mosques.[4] The thinking was that if speakers could be criminalised for uttering words that offended or hurt others, especially if their words led to violence, we would have better 'social cohesion'.

Not true. Social cohesion derives from open debate, not by protecting individuals and groups from being hurt! Whether they are hurt or not lies in their own hands, their reactions to what they see or hear.

Censoring speakers' views, legislating for silence, has never worked in history. If the activists for the abolition of slavery or apartheid or for women to be given the right to vote had been silenced we would still be living in the dark ages!

It's not healthy or helpful to wrap up social activists, of whatever hue, in protective bubbles, so they won't be hurt! Nor is it healthy or helpful to want laws that force people to keep quiet and follow the crowd, especially if they have alternative views that might be helpful to the progress and wellbeing of that crowd.

Anyway, who would decide what is 'hateful' speech? Who would be the moral arbiters? Who knows best what we should or should not say? The police? The courts? Politicians?

In July 2021 a central Wellington billboard was removed because the transgender movement regarded it as offensive. The billboard simply displayed the Oxford English Dictionary definition of 'woman' – adult, human female. It came from the Speak Up for Women movement, whose aim is to 'advocate for the sex-based rights of women and girls'. But it was criticised as 'misgendering' and 'dehumanising' and 'potentially dangerous' by the transgender movement. Potentially?

It is impossible, under any pretext, to regard such a statement as hate speech. In itself it was harmless. Just a definition. But the activists read into it a wider significance.

But the Speak Up for Women had further problems. The Palmerston North, Dunedin and Christchurch City Councils had cancelled their bookings or refused to allow them to hold public meetings. However, they were forced to reverse their decisions after a High Court ruling that "the cancellation decision was not a rational and reasonable limitation on rights."[5]

But it gets worse. In 2023 a woman, who happened to be a criminal defence lawyer, was arrested, handcuffed and locked in a police van for peacefully holding a counter sign during a pro-Palestinian protest march. There was no breaking of the law, no incitement to violence. She was just standing there.

In the same year a high school teacher was deregistered because he refused to use the preferred pronouns for a fourteen-year-old girl who was becoming a boy, because it was against his Christian beliefs.

It's unbelievable that this sort of thing is happening in a modern democracy. It smacks of Orwellianism.

The present laws provide enough restrictions on speech-making, without resorting to specific hate speech legislation. It's already illegal to libel someone and to incite hostility or discriminate against people based on their sex, marital status, religious beliefs, disability, age or sexual orientation.

The task of Orwell's thought police, in his imaginary totalitarian state was to punish the thoughts and sayings of which big brother disapproved.[6] Using a variety of methods, including surveillance, censorship and informants, people were punished if they contravened in any way the policies of the totalitarian state.

Not many people know that for a period the New Zealand police were being trained to detect hate speech and make arrests. Apparently, they have now 'doubled down' on that approach.

It's somewhat frightening to think what speech or behaviour might be considered 'hate'. If, for example, opinions about gender, marriage or racism, which differ from how the police define them, are targeted we could see many wrongful arrests of decent people who simply wish to express their point of view.

I don't belong to any political or pseudo political group. I simply listen to and read about what is happening in society around me. I have to honestly confess I am somewhat fearful of the future health of Kiwi society if we fail to halt the present attacks on the freedom to hold and utter one's personal opinions.

How free is speech? Not as free as it used to be.

[1] Radio New Zealand, 24.3.23
[2] Nicolette Levy KC, RNZ 24.3.23
[3] https://www.wikipedia.org
[4] 'Woke' is a slang term used by right-wing politicians to describe those

who are extremely sensitive to social inequalities such as sexism, racism, and the rights of the marginalised.
5   Whitmore v. Palmerston North City Council, 13 July, 2021
6   Orwell, George, *1984,* Secker and Warburg, 1949

10
Truth Decay

I was involved in politics once.

A reporter of a metropolitan newspaper phoned me for my response to a certain matter. I told him I had nothing to say. Despite his persistent questioning I still had no comment to make. Imagine my surprise and angst when I discovered myself on the front page, saying things I'd never said. The smart reporter had interpreted my silence as meaning something he conjectured it meant and had put words into my mouth. It was all false, untrue, lies – 'fake news'.

It wasn't the first time either. I've often been misinterpreted or misrepresented, not only by news sources but also by various individuals or groups who try to fit what I've said or espoused into their own thinking agendas, their concept of the world, thereby falsifying truth.

Wikipedia defines 'truth' as 'the property of being in accord with fact or reality' and it 'is usually held to be the opposite of falsehood.[1] Truth is objective, not opinion. It can be verified. In other words, it is not imaginary. It is constructive and leads to positive action. Lies have a negative impact.

In fact, we rely on truth – our perception of what is real – for our daily living and progress. It is basic, not only to our perception of the physical things around us but also to life principles. For example, it is true we can never please everyone. It is true we will all suffer loss of some sort and the weather keeps changing. It is true that water is the key liquid for cleansing, but if we falsely believe it is vinegar or acid we're in trouble.

Truth eroded

My stance in this book is that the concept of truth has been progressively eroded. We don't hold it in high honour as we used to. Commonly held views of what is factual or real are being increasingly misrepresented or outrightly falsified, mainly for political or commercial gain.

A recent, glaring example is the claim by the former president of the United States that he won the 2020 election, when every verifiable investigation showed he didn't.

Such misrepresentation often applies to historical events or documents and to moral principles as well. The holocaust in World War 2 was real, despite all the deniers. The present world climate change is a well attested scientific fact, not a myth. The traditional moral truth that it is wrong to steal still applies, not the sort of morality that says "I have a right. What's yours is mine".

Falsifying truth is a key factor in bringing about social disunity and polarisation, as citizens become confused about what to believe.

In his book *Post Truth*, Lee McIntyre notes that "The selective use of facts to prop up one's position, and the complete rejection of facts that do not, seems part and parcel of creating the new post-truth reality."[2]

"Always tell the truth", we consistently told our children. Why? It wasn't that we just wanted to rear honest, upright children. It was also because telling lies leads to negative gossip, a distortion of what is real, and possible trouble, or even danger. People trusted those who told the truth. It was the honest thing to do.

The spreading of false information (lies) or propaganda has always been a key tactic of those who want to manipulate others to their way of thinking, and it is spreading. It has been used widely in war and politics. Politicians are very much aware that public opinion is shaped more by emotional appeals than by facts.

The Russian-Ukrainian conflict presents lots of examples. Russia's President Putin started a war, based on a lie. He said he invaded Ukraine because Ukraine was led by neo-Nazis who were committing genocide on their own people. Absolute nonsense. Ukraine's president is a Jew, not a Nazi, and so is the Ukrainian Prime Minister.

George W. Bush, former president of the United States, also started a war based on a lie. Along with millions of others I watched his former Secretary of State, Colin Powell, present a case to the United Nations Security Council for the invasion of Iraq. Among other things he alleged Iraq was harbouring weapons of mass destruction and creating biological weapons. The invasion found none! "He later admitted that his speech contained substantial inaccuracies."[3]

Truth matters

When leaders speak, people listen.

In recent years a new phenomenon has arisen – fact-checking. This is now necessary to enable us to know whether or not our leaders are in touch with reality.

Since World War 2, with the liberalisation of society, lies, misinformation, disinformation and conspiracies have blunted truth telling. The advent of the internet, digital technology and social media have served this trend well.

There has been an undermining of once-held cultural and societal views and a cynical challenging of evidence presented by scientists and experts. What was once considered real is not viewed as real anymore.

Whether something is true or not now largely depends on a person's subjective feelings and experience rather than on objective reality. "It's true for me." So, people espouse different 'truths' for the same topic or event depending on their situation and bias.

There may well be different opinions but not alternative truths! And some people actually believe blatant untruths as truth!

The Covid19 pandemic clearly illustrated the trend. There were many untruths circulating. I came face to face with a number of them. Distrust of inoculations was widespread. Some of my friends believed the new vaccines were designed by pharmaceutical companies to harm, not cure. It was difficult to reason with them, so fixed were they on what was obviously not true.

Many thought Covid19 could be prevented simply by gargling with salt water, or injecting bleach or ivermectin into the body or spraying it with chlorine. This sort of advice flew in the face of scientific proof. Individuals thought they knew better than proven research. Apart from gargling, the other so-called remedies could be harmful or dangerous.

After I had a Covid19 injection my neighbour visited me and asked if I could roll up my sleeve. He placed a coin over the place where the needle had been inserted. It immediately fell on to the driveway. Did he think I had been injected with a magnetic microchip?

Conspiracy

Conspiracy theories like this are not new. A number have gained traction over time. Some people believed that the 1969 moon landing was fake, that Princess Diana's death was not an accident, and that Bayer aspirin spread HIV.

It has always puzzled me why people, including some well-known personalities, believe ardently in such untruths, why they endorse the opposite of what has been scientifically proven.

Psychologists tell us there are a number of reasons. When people feel alienated and marginalised, they can readily fear big organisations are against them. Grasping new and different ideas helps them feel safe and in control of new and important information of which, they think, the bulk of the population is ignorant. Verifiable evidence becomes suspect. They use the internet to spread their new-found knowledge, and don't feel disadvantaged anymore. They live in a different reality from the norm.

Consequences

The deliberate spreading of inaccurate information has a negative impact on society. It poses a threat to freedom. It so easily spreads confusion, conflict, hate, extreme ideas, polarisation of society and violence. It erodes confidence and trust among friends and in social discourse. It stunts progress, and throws suspicion on causes and institutions that were formerly respected. The line between fact and fiction becomes blurred. As a result, it is difficult to have robust and informed debate.

How is a healthy respect for truth to be restored?

First, we need to challenge untruth when we see or hear it.

Second, we all need to check reliable sources for what we say, especially on social media. Opinion based entirely on personal bias, without well-founded backup, can be socially damaging.

As an interested observer I find myself continually comparing different media reports to find out what's really going on around me. I keep questioning what is real and what is not, so I can build an accurate picture.

Third, perhaps the teaching of critical thinking should receive greater emphasis in our schools. How do we recognise the difference between fact and opinion? How do we process information and determine what is false? How should we handle social media? How do we distinguish truth from untruth?

Fourth, there needs to be greater co-operation among those organisations, including the media, that broadcast information to the public.

Fifth, communities need to find general agreement on basic truths if they want social cohesion.

Sixth, open debate and tolerance of diverse viewpoints is to be encouraged, if society is to progress in a functioning democracy. It's vital to listen to all points of view in order to reach common ground.

Truth cannot be determined by government edict, that is, from the top down. It is to be hoped that we never get an Orwellian-type government-controlled

Ministry of Truth where facts and records are altered to fit party or government propaganda and doctrine.

Someone once said that truth is the first casualty in the establishment of a totalitarian state.

Does truth matter? Definitely. It's dangerous to avoid reality.

[1]   https://en.wikipedia.org
[2]   *Post Truth,* Lee McIntyre, MIT Press, 2018
[3]   https://en.wikipeda.org

11
Wanted – More Wisdom

The world's in a mess. Leaders with insight and vision are urgently needed.

There are thousands of politicians, but few statespersons.

There are many fools, but few who are wise.

With each passing decade everything seems to get messier. This is not merely the thinking of one ageing Kiwi. Other ageing Kiwis agree. So do the experts.

Carme Colomina, senior researcher, at the Barcelona Centre for International Affairs, says we began 2024 in an "increasingly diverse and disorganised world." She said, "The erosion of international norms is more acute than ever, and events become more unpredictable."[1]

The Centre noted that in 2023 world political violence increased by 27%, with 32 armed conflicts around the world at the moment, and 114 million people displaced worldwide, seven million of them in Sudan alone.[2]

There is a disregard of international law, threats to international security, widespread disinformation and massive economic inequality.

Populist authoritarians and far right extremists are on the rise in every continent and democracies are in trouble with political polarisation. Civil dissent and protest movements are being restricted. The USA is not the only country where results of democratic voting have been challenged. Instability and violence relating to electoral processes is spreading. Add to these global challenges the unpredictable massive climate events.

The United Nations Security Council is paralysed by ongoing vetoes. Many fine words are spoken about ceasefires and peace but consequent action seems non-existent.

In a globalised world New Zealand is no longer isolated. World influencers are at work here too. Dr Bryce Edwards says, "Toxicity and disinformation are becoming a big part of New Zealand politics. And much of this relates to debates about ethnicity, race and racism."[3]

He writes of a "serious populist discontent" arising in New Zealand, quoting surveys that show a "'high level of discontent and anti-establishment feeling'" and a "'declining trust and faith in political and public institutions'".

Writer and political commentator, Jacqui Van Der Kaay, draws attention to the New Zealand Election Study for the 2023 election. The survey found that 35% of New Zealanders disagreed that politicians behave with great integrity.[4] Various polls have consistently shown that politicians are among the least trustworthy professionals.

This is not surprising when we reflect on the political behaviour of members of all parties in recent years – personal scandals, bullying, increasing anti-personal venom, undeclared conflicts of interests, verbal abuse of staff, shoplifting…

An Otago University survey reports that 98% of MPs say they have been harassed in various ways.[5]

The fact that they might well work hard over long hours out of public view is no excuse. In a democracy we expect our leaders to show decorum and respect. What we see far too often is a lot of ego tripping, heavy biases and intolerance of opposing views.

Where are our true leaders, our statesmen and women, our people of vision and wisdom?

Personal

As I've journeyed through life, now and again I've wandered off the pathway, as we all do. Wise people have counselled me back on track. Sometimes it was encouragement from a parent or relative, sometimes a pertinent comment from a teacher or a minister of the cloth, but sometimes it was a word from a stranger, a casual acquaintance at a chance meeting.

I've met many who talk a lot, yet say little.

I've met many who think they know a lot but their thoughts are shallow.

I've met some who do know a lot but share sparingly.

At times, however, I've met someone who knows a lot and shares gems of insight that help one through the complexities of life. They may not be called 'heroes' but they are certainly models to follow.

Such people are precious. Their wide experience of life helps them understand the human condition. Their positive contribution helps individuals and society progress.

They are wise.

We need wisdom

The world desperately needs more of these sorts of people – more wisdom. The predominance of the unwise is producing confusion and polarisation across the globe.

Wise people have a mature understanding of life built on wide experiences. They are open to other people's points of view and flexible in their thinking. They spend time reflecting on life and its challenges, learning from their mistakes. They're always questioning their own views and those of others.

As a result, they lead meaningful, balanced lives, are positive in outlook and work for the common good. They encourage kindness.

We urgently need such people.

I've always considered wise people as those who are older than me but one doesn't necessarily become wiser as one gets older. Some of the elderly are foolish and indiscreet.

Gems of wisdom often come "'out of the mouths of babes'".[6] At times the young and inexperienced can be remarkably wise, surprising everyone. Despite their age and innocence children occasionally utter profound truths. For example, amidst a heated family argument a two-year-old is heard to yell, "Everyone should be friends." A father might be somewhat depressed after a failure at work, and his little daughter says, "You should be happy because you're alive." How true.

But generally, the growing of wisdom takes time and experience. It can't be learnt from books. There's no academic course.

Walter Moss, Professor Emeritus of history at East Michigan University said, when writing about USA Congressional elections: "We want our leaders to exercise political wisdom."[7]

We all shout "Amen." So, why aren't such people leading us?

Perhaps too much power is concentrated in the hands of the economic elite who govern mainly for vocal lobby groups. Perhaps our leaders lack understanding of the real needs of the silent majority. Perhaps not enough time is taken to hear all points of view, so vital in a democracy.

Wise and visionary leaders have firm ethical values, such as honesty and accountability. They lead by example and foster strong relationships.

The ancient Greek philosopher, Aristotle, believed the true student of politics should study virtue above all things. By 'virtue' he meant attributes like self-discipline, humility, truthfulness and honesty.

Empathy is so often missing in our leaders. So, too, a sense of humour, tolerance and a willingness to compromise. Professor Moss points out the scarcity of humility in the United States Congress. Instead, what we get is "in-your-face assertiveness".

Maybe our problem in Aotearoa New Zealand lies in a closer scrutiny of the character of candidates, the need for greater accountability from politicians via a four-year parliamentary term and agreement on a core set of values.

The quality of a nation's leadership matters.

Wanted – more wisdom.

1. The Barcelona Centre for International Affairs (CIDOB) is a Spanish think tank headquartered in Barcelona, devoted to research in the field of international relations.
2. https://en.wikipedia.org
3. Dr Bryce Edwards, political analyst Victoria University, Democracy Project, 27.5.24
4. Article: *Politicians Need to Lift Their Game*, 16.9.24. See *Back on Track,* ed Stephen Levine, Victoria University, 2024
5. Otago University Survey, April, 2024, Susanna Every-Palmer, Oliver Hansby, Justin Barry-Walsh
6. *The Bible*, Psalm 8:2
7. Walter Moss, *What is True Political Wisdom? A Primer for the 2012 Election*, essay, 5.3.12

12

Spirituality and Politics

As soon as I put that title at the top of the page, I heard cries of "Keep religion out of politics. State and Church should be separate"!

I'm not advocating anything of the sort. I'm not suggesting religion, any religion, be involved in parliamentary matters. I'm not suggesting Members of Parliament become Christians or Moslems or Sikhs.

Spirituality and religion are two different animals although they can, obviously, be connected. The latter is an organisation established by human beings, with rules and regulations, for the growing and practising of faith. The former doesn't necessarily need such an organisation but it can be practised anywhere at any time. People can grow spiritually without being involved in a religion.

While spirituality used to be associated with all kinds of religious and pseudo religious groups, it has a much broader definition today. Because of our increasing diversity, and the decline of traditional religion, there are many spiritualities.

I've personally met many people, including friends, who don't go near a church, mosque or temple but declare they have or are seeking their own spirituality. They enjoy exploring the meaning of life and their interconnectedness to others. They try to develop a oneness with nature and to the universe, through a whole range of practices, without any reference to God or gods.

An increasing number of people are not churchgoers. In fact, only 31.2 per cent of New Zealanders claim to be Christian and, of them, only 12% attend a church regularly. Over half the population say they have no religion (51.6%).[1] New Zealand is very much a secular state.

Thousands of 'lost' churchgoers have now found comfort in developing their own spirituality. Indeed, Professor Peter Lineham says, "Spirituality has replaced religion in our society; formal religion is now seen as a very negative force by many in our society, but spirituality is seen as a way for people to connect with something deeper."[2]

It's difficult to discover how many Kiwis follow their own spirituality rather than belong to a religion. Research on this topic is somewhat limited. However, a random survey of over 2,040 adults confirmed that despite declining church attendance spiritual experiences have increased. In fact, 45.2% of the sample said "they have their own way of connecting with God without churches or religious services."[3]

All this suggests considerable spiritual searching is going on, which indicates an emptiness of soul among the population and a desire to complement a materialistic, secular existence. The human being is not just a two-dimensional figure, not just a physical and sensual being. There's a third dimension, one of spirituality.

This is why we have witnessed a number of spiritual-type groups and practices arise in the past few decades, with a focus on self-improvement, a deeper connection with the natural world, and an emphasis on mystical knowledge and holistic healing. This is why 'mind, body, and spirit' shelves in Whitcoulls have exploded, leaving overt Christian material apologetically gathering dust in the bottom right-hand corner.

More spirituality in politics

Why do I mention this widespread interest in spirituality? Simply because I think it's time politicians and community leaders paid more attention to the spiritual component of people in their legislation and decision-making. It would seem basic commonsense that by doing so the recipients of such decisions would be more satisfied and happier.

Professor Richard Egan of Otago University argued for spiritual awareness to be fostered "at every level of society, from our political directions to our individual choices." He believes "spirituality is a missing factor in the way we structure our society, from politics to health and education.[4]

What does this mean?

In terms of politics it means that decision-makers need to consider the effects of their decisions on the whole person. Do their decisions help citizens find meaning and purpose? Do they make people any happier? Do they help them connect with others in community and with the natural world around them, as Māori do with wairuatanga? Do their decisions cultivate core human values like empathy and tolerance, and foster hope?

Politics is about organising and administrating our society so that it works for the good of the people in a rational and just way. Unfortunately, this is not always the case. Mistakes are made. Our leaders, both nationally and locally, often spend too much time 'playing politics', building personal egos, combatting each other, scoring partisan points, wasting taxpayers' money, constantly with eyes on the next election.

More spirituality in politics would require a different tone and approach. It would require wider consultation, certainly with different cultures, not just the tangata whenua. It would present a vision of the future and plan long-term rather than be dictated to by the election cycle. It would seek what the people really want and need, rather than relying on lobby group pressure.

People would form the focal centre, not party doctrine or personal political agendas. Spirituality would respect individuals as unique, not simply as objects of legislation or receivers of a benefit or nameless members of some group or other. Their freedom and human rights would be respected.

Spirituality in politics would foster the unity of diverse groups. Partisanship would not be an issue and the democratic principle would apply at all levels. It would promote respect for the law and ethics and encourage a spirit of empathy and action for good.

It may well be that some of these principles are now applied to the making of certain laws but I am suggesting a new, perhaps more radical, approach, one that envisages a person holistically.

Research, especially in the health field, has shown that addressing the spiritual nature of people produces benefits, such as better mental health, better coping with stress, improved wellbeing, and increased social support.[5]

Applying spirituality principles to the political field might need some research and serious thought but if positive outcomes are achieved then a healthier society would be the winner.

To some readers, using spirituality principles to improve the political machine might seem somewhat utopian. How is it possible for a government to consider the spirituality input into decision-making when they have so much else to worry about? However, if there's a will nothing is impossible.

"Spirituality is not the renunciation of life; it is the art of living fully."[6]

[1] NZ Census 2023

[2] Article in NZ Herald, 31.12.005 by C. Harvey

[3] *Spirituality and Religion in the Lives of New Zealanders,* F.Vaccarino, H. Kavan, P. Gendall, in International Journal of Religion and Spirituality in Society, January 2011

[4] Article in *Journal of Pain and Symptom Management*, Vol. 57, Issue 5, 2019

[5] See, for example, the Harvard T.H.Chan School of Public Health, the NZ Health Research Council, and the Otago University Social and Behavioural Research Unit

[6] Acharya Prashant, Indian author and speaker

13

Please Don't Call Me Racist

'Racist' is a label used far too liberally by a wide cross-section of people and groups.

Even genuine attempts to improve race relations are often so tagged. The effect is a curtailment of robust debate.

Personally, I've often hesitated to discuss race relations in any shape or form, for fear of being pigeon-holed as a racist. I've been reluctant to ask key questions or comment upon, let alone criticise, any outworking of the Treaty of Waitangi or decisions relating to the general welfare of Māori.

However, I've been thinking lately about the social and political divisions caused by confusion over the meaning of the two versions of this country's founding document. And I am not the only one. Many people of all ethnicities, are perplexed, and the confusion seems to be increasing as the years pass.

As an ordinary, third-generation Kiwi why do I feel so stressed about recent Māori/Government relationships? Why do I feel concerned about the rhetoric, the name-calling, and the increasing polarisation between sections of the community? It's all negative and endangers sound bicultural relationships.

Perhaps it's because greater media coverage has made me more aware. Perhaps it's because the chatter of the people and groups around me has challenged me to think. Or, perhaps, it's because certain words and concepts lack clear definition.

I sense that the silent majority of Kiwis share my concern and confusion. They tire of the situation and simply disconnect. However, the questions keep arising. After 184 years since the signing of the Treaty we are still asking what it all means; while experts continue to debate their differences.

What, indeed, are the principles? What does Māori self-determination really mean? When will all historic injustices be resolved? Who owns our fresh water? Why can't we sort out the foreshore and seabed ownership?

We now live in a diverse society. What does the Treaty mean to other cultures? If we are to have a unified, progressive future these cultures also need to be apprised of Treaty implications if they are to become active and understanding participants.

More Asians now live in New Zealand than Māori and, by 2043, they will make up 26% of the population. Most are of Indian or Chinese descent. Pacific Islanders are 266,000 of the population. There are 73,000

Filipinos and about as many from Middle Eastern, Latin American and African heritage.[1]

Are they all on board with Treaty arrangements and definitions?

Personal credentials

What right have I to write about this?

My personal history compels me.

Like many pakeha New Zealanders, especially those born in the mid-to-south of this country, my upbringing was monocultural.

As a young youth leader, I was given the opportunity to spend a week living with a Māori pastor and his family in the small settlement of Waima, alongside the Waima River, south-west of Kaikohe. A Wesleyan Mission Station had been established there in 1858. Each day we travelled on horseback to visit Māori kainga (homes). Needless to say, the week was enlightening and made a lasting impression on me.

As a young secondary school teacher in the Waikato, Auckland and Northland, I endeavoured to relate to my Māori students as well as I could. I started learning te reo (the language), and finding opportunities to stay on marae to study Māori protocol. Later, as a high school principal I worked with local kaumatua to establish a whare wananga (house of learning), complete with tukutuku panels. A teacher of Māori language was appointed. Our kapa haka group toured Northland schools, and I spoke on a number of marae.

My knowledge and pronunciation of the language and understanding of protocol was improving as I welcomed people on to our school marae, and spoke at various functions, including tangihanga (funerals). In fact, when I became a church pastor, I led several tangihanga, one deep in the heart of the King Country.

When I retired from my principalship I was honoured by being appointed a pakeha kaumatua (elder), which meant I was able to stand on that particular turangawaeae (place, home base) without invitation.

A few years later, I was able to take a course in te reo and was examined orally by the first Māori Governor-General, Sir Paul Reeves, passing with honours!

Let no-one doubt that I have endeavoured to identify with the aspirations of my Māori brothers and sisters and tried to do what I can to advance the cause. I am not a racist!

In my lifetime there has been an ever-increasing Māori involvement in New Zealand social, political, cultural and sporting life.

For example, there are now 33 Māori Members of Parliament across all parties, and a Māori political party. Over 40 councils have Māori wards.

The Māori economy is "vibrant, varied and rapidly

growing".[2] Over the last ten years, the Māori asset base has also grown at a significantly faster rate than the overall economy.[3] Willie Jackson, former Labour Minister of Māori Development, said the expected worth of the Māori economy would be $100 billion by 2030.[4]

By 2018 the Government had settled 73 Treaty claims mainly for land confiscations at a cost of $2.24 billion.[5]

The teaching and learning of Māori language have grown. There are now 72 kura kaupapa (language immersion schools), over 400 kohanga reo (language nests for young children), and 182 secondary schools that offer the language. The media are using te reo often and public signage is becoming more bicultural.

New Zealanders have every reason to be proud of the achievements of Māori in sport and the arts, both here and overseas, with heroes like Dame Lisa Carrington, Suzie Bates, Wynton Rufer, Noeline Taurua, Michael Campbell and numerous All Blacks.

Awareness of Māori tikanga (culture) is spreading.

Concerns

Nevertheless, there are a number of concerns.

The man or woman in the street can't understand what's happening, and neither can a number of my Māori friends. They hear the rhetoric, see the hikoi (march), feel the frustration and anger, but are confused and not drawn into the conversation. While some people may be upset by thousands of protesters marching; peaceful protests, of whatever type, are important in a democracy.

Some of the language used is not appreciated, such as that of the co-leader of Te Pati Māori when he addressed the hikoi in front of parliament on 19 November, 2024: "When will we start to lead ourselves to our own liberation? Today the revolution starts."

To many Kiwis this is scary stuff. 'Liberation?' 'Revolution?' Many are alarmed by talk of self-determination and co-governance, and the possibility of a separate Māori parliament. They don't believe anyone should own the country's foreshore, seabed, and freshwater. They tire of hearing about the injustices of the past and the sins of their colonialist forbears. And they are exasperated by the apparent continual demands for more.

Today, it's the Treaty principles that are hitting the headlines. "What are they?" they ask. Did Māori cede sovereignty or not? Are Māori to run their own affairs or not? If we are supposed to be a partnership then what form should it take? It is not surprising, therefore, that 46% of the population supported the proposal to clarify the principles.[6]

The debate about principles is not new. Many people are probably unaware that the principles are spelt out by the Waitangi Tribunal, the courts and Government, when they make decisions at various times. In 1987

Sir Robin Cooke made a ruling on Treaty principles in the Court of Appeal. He was clear that the Crown has sovereignty, in exchange for the protection of rangatiratanga (self-determination). In 1989 the fourth Labour Government adopted five principles for Crown action on the Treaty.

The disbanding of the Māori Health Authority is another issue of the moment. Some view it as an 'attack' on Treaty principles, but the Government sees it as a political tactic to deal with the issue from a different perspective – not through a nationwide, bureaucratic structure but, using the same resources, via more targeted, local methods. It's debatable what approach would produce better outcomes.

What now?

If our nation is to become less confused and more unified over racial matters, open debate is important for understanding and making progress. We should not be afraid of it. Let's stop talking past each other and clarify basic issues now, not in another 180 years. It's time to cease the filibustering and embark on more serious conversations. It's time to work collaboratively towards mutually acceptable outcomes.

The terminology used needs to be clearly defined. When we speak of rangatiratanga, for example, what does that mean in practical terms? What's the difference between 'ownership' and 'customary rights?' Who has what rights?

It's been 50 years since the Waitangi Tribunal was established. Perhaps it's time to hasten the redress of past grievances and work on the nature of real partnership.

[1] Stats NZ, June 2024
[2] Christian Hawkesby, Assistant Reserve Bank Governor, 6 May 2021
[3] NZ Herald, 8 June, 2022
[4] New Zealand Herald, 16 November, 2022
[5] htttps://teara.govt.nz
[6] Curia poll, 4.10.24

14

Is The End Really Nigh?

My thinking about life takes place in a variety of places. Most often I sit in the corner of a café, drinking a soy milk cappuccino, plugged into the cafe's WiFi. Sometimes I sit in bed with my laptop. Thoughts come as I sleep, watch television, read the paper, or at any time of the day while embarked on varied projects.

I write this as I sit in my Mazda3 looking out over a full tide in Tauranga's Memorial Park, New Zealand. It's a somewhat grey day but, nevertheless, a very beautiful scene. So peaceful.

Surely nothing could disrupt such tranquillity. I feel so safe here. Maybe it's a fool's paradise. Life has taught me that you can take little for granted. It's so unpredictable.

My mind jumps to places where it's far from peaceful – the wars in Ukraine, the Middle East and the centre of Africa. I focus on the plight of Palestinian refugees, the migration of thousands of people from their homelands, and the millions suffering poverty and famine. I wince at the inhumane treatment by humans of other humans, such as the attitude to women in Afghanistan or the Chinese treatment of the Uighurs.

I wonder if conflicts and human misery will ever end. I wonder if human beings will ever cease bombing and maiming other human beings? Perhaps never, if the dark side of human nature is never reformed but allowed to operate unchallenged.

I've often joked that the older one gets the messier the world seems to become. No joke. After decades of reasonably close observation of, and involvement in, the social/political scene, I believe I have cause to be alarmed. Nothing is as it used to be. Yes, we have made progress, some of it good, but much of it not so good.

Extinct?

One day, I think, the world as we know it will end. Human beings will be no more, just like the moas and dinosaurs and hundreds of species which have become, or are in the process of becoming, extinct. I wonder if human beings will follow the same path, because of what they have done, and the way they have treated each other and their environment. Humans might eventually destroy the very civilisation they've spent thousands of years building up.

This is not a new thought. History is a teacher. Regional civilisations have come and gone in the past, because of economic collapse, climate change, wars, disease, or natural disasters, usually a combination of a number of factors. The Roman Empire, for example, folded because it over-reached itself and became too greedy. In the end it couldn't cope with its complexities.

The Central American Aztecs were wiped out by rivals and disease. And the Sumerians of Mesopotamia were conquered by the Persians. Centuries later there are signs that our present world order embodies a number of factors that could bring about a wider major societal collapse, if not human extinction.

Professor Toby Ord of Oxford University says that "For the first time in humanity's history we now have the capacity to destroy ourselves."[1]

Professor Schellnhuber, director emeritus of the Potsdam Institute for Climate Impact Research said that if we continue down the present path "there is a very big risk that we will just end our civilisation."[2]

Australian scientist, Dr Graham Turner, has been warning about civilisation collapse for decades, based on his modelling research.

Climate scientist Will Steffen, Emeritus Professor at the Australian National University, said "we are already deep into the trajectory towards collapse."[3]

The United Nations Secretary-General, Antonio Guterres, believes "We are on the edge of an abyss, and moving in the wrong directions…The world must wake up."[4]

Risks to civilisation

The world is very unstable. Scientists, philosophers, writers and some world leaders are increasingly propounding the 'existential risks' humanity faces.

They agree a collapse of human civilisation won't be brought about by any one of these risks unless there's a massive nuclear holocaust. Our demise will be caused by a combination of factors over decades of growing crises and instability. And it probably won't be the results of natural disasters themselves but by human-made factors – self-destruction.

(i) War has become a major disease. There are a number of reasons why nations fight each other – ideological, economic, nationalistic, the desire for revenge, territorial gain, autocratic leadership, ethnic and religious violence. I am now absolutely convinced that violence simply causes more violence, and solves little.

What good results from war? Nothing, as far as I can see, except huge profits for munitions manufacturers. Millions of human beings are killed, maimed, or displaced as refugees, especially civilians and mainly women and children. Homes are destroyed. Economies suffer.

Peace efforts are slow. There is always a lot of talk but little action. The United Nations seems powerless.

As I write, the situation in the Middle East is tense, on the verge of a major conflict. The Russia/Ukraine conflict is exploding. Fighting is ongoing in Yemen, Syria, Sudan, Myanmar... In fact, 32 countries are presently at war.[5]

A total nuclear war is now far more possible than when Hiroshima and Nagasaki were bombed in World War 2. Then, only the USA had a nuclear arsenal. Now, eight nations have sophisticated nuclear weaponry, including intercontinental missiles and weapons unheard of during the second world war.

We live on the brink.

(ii) Climate change has a high priority on the United Nations' agenda, as the world's resources of water, fisheries, forests and land are being depleted. Sir David Attenborough believes the degradation of our environment could lead to the collapse of civilisation and the extinction of much of the natural world.

The 8,000-page IPCC Report, compiled by hundreds of the world's top climate scientists, was released in March 2023. It provides sober reading. For example, the last decade was warmer than any previous period and the sea level has been rising faster than in any prior century for the past 3,000 years.

Climate impacts on people and ecosystems are more widespread and severe than expected and all countries are affected. At the 2024 Pacific Islands Forum, Antonio Guterres referred to rising sea levels as 'a global SOS'. It was a 'devastating' picture.[6]

Despite regular world conferences, such as the one in Dubai at the end of 2023, progress in curbing carbon emissions has been slow. A number of countries were not supportive of moving away from the use of fossil fuels.

For this risk to be managed huge financial investment is needed.

(iii) We face global economic collapse, brought about by the need to support a burgeoning world population, high consumption lifestyles, decline in natural resources, a stretched environment and massive inequalities within and between nations, especially the widening gap between rich and poor. The top 10% of global income earners are responsible for almost as much total greenhouse gas emissions as the bottom 90%. Half the world's population live on less than $3 a day.

Waves of migrations of people from failing economies will continue to put pressure on more stable states.

(iv) There will be further global pandemics. HIV/AIDS killed 36 million people, Covid19 killed seven million, but in the Spanish flu of 1918 fifty million died. Scientists indicate that as the planet continues warming up, as we continue to deforest, as habitats collapse, as global travel increases and as key antibiotics become ineffective there is the possibility of more viruses transmitting from animals to humans.

We somehow eventually managed the worst effects of Covid19 but another pandemic could be far worse. At the 2024 World Economic Forum the World Health Organisation estimated the next pandemic could be twenty times worse than Covid19.[7]

(v) Natural disasters — fires, floods, earthquakes, hurricanes, and famines — are plaguing humankind with increasing regularity and intensity, some of almost apocalyptic proportions. And let's not forget that there's always the possibility of a catastrophic asteroid strike or a series of solar tsunamis.

(vi) Cyber weapons are becoming increasingly sophisticated and could hold whole nations to ransom, with artificial intelligence playing a major part.

Well-known historian and author Yuval Harari has just published a new book, *Nexus*. He highlights existential threats, especially new technologies driven by artificial intelligence. New technologies could well annihilate us.[8]

Timing

If human beings become extinct it will be a matter of when and how, not if.

No scientist, politician or philosopher can determine with any accuracy when human society might collapse, although some have tried.

Eminent Australian Professor Frank Fenner predicts humans will probably be extinct within 100 years, because of over-population, environmental destruction and climate change.[9] He says more people means fewer resources and a lot more wars over food.

This same article compared what's happening now to what happened on Easter Island – once a pristine tropical island but as the population exploded forests were wiped out and animals became extinct. Civilisation there started to collapse about 1600 and disappeared altogether mid-19th century.

Biologists tell us half the Earth's species could be extinct by 2050.[10]

A Melbourne-based think tank reported that there is a likelihood human civilization will come to an end by 2050![11]

What can we do about it?

While I confess much of the above sounds depressing all is not gloom and doom. There is always hope. If we act now and do the right things we could exist for thousands of years. If we don't, our continued existence is problematic.

Many individuals and groups want to do something, but what – apart from recycling our household waste – can we do to make any difference? Trying to reduce my own carbon footprint seems of little use unless everyone does so. Even so, our combined personal actions, while noble, would be scarcely noticeable in the face of world-wide global needs.

I could simply bury my head in the sand and ignore the risks, pretending they're not there – but they are. I could assume any threat of human society collapsing doesn't concern me, for I've had a full life. But that's selfish. What about my children and their children?

So, we rely on our political leaders, but do they have the will?

The science exists to change our course, and human beings can be very creative and innovative if they use new technologies wisely and discover different renewable energies, and sustainable options in agriculture and industry. There seems to be no limit to human potential, given the right incentives.

Three actions are necessary.

(i) We desperately need long-term planning and solutions but, unfortunately, we tend to think only short-term, satisfying our immediate needs, maintaining an existence, earning an income, caring for family.

This attitude was crystallised at the beginning of the movie *Vice*, about former USA vice-president Dick Cheney: "As the world becomes more and more confusing we tend to focus on the things that are right there in front of us while ignoring the massive forces that actually change and shape our lives."

The political excuse is that it's very difficult and too expensive to think far into the future. There are too many variables to alter or change our best-laid plans.

(ii) Long-term planning requires dynamic leadership, leadership with the will and determination to make brave decisions about the future of the planet.

Richard Fisher, managing director of the BBC.com features sites recently wrote: "It's possible that we are at one of the most precarious points of human history, Yet I worry at our power to destroy ourselves is radically outstripping our wisdom and foresight."[12] Toby Ord made a similar observation in *Precipice*.

(iii) A collective effort is required.

With strong world leadership we can work together to manage the risks. The world is presently too fragmented. Interconnectedness is the key to a better future, that is, global co-operation. Unfortunately, a number of key countries are becoming more nationalistic.

Together, we need to work for peace, carbon-free environments, sustainable futures and greater innovations.

Is the end really nigh? Christians believe that human beings will have to suffer a period of 'tribulation' before the end comes. Are we in that period now?[13]

When the end does come, they believe there will be 'a new heaven and a new Earth'.

I wonder.

---

[1] *The Precipice: Existential Risk and the Future of Humanity,* T.Ord, Hachette, 2020

[2] Quoted in *Voice of Action* 8.6.2020

[3] Quoted by Asher Moses, 7.6.20 *Collapse of Civilisation is the Most Likely Outcome*

[4] United Nations speech, 21 September, 2021

[5] www.worldpopulationreview.com

[6] New Zealand Herald, 28.8.2024

[7] www.newsnationnow.com

8   Harari, Yuval, *Nexus,* Penguin, 2024
9   *The Australian*, Lin Edwards, 23 June, 2010
10 www.worlbank.org
11 Breakthrough National Centre for Climate Restoration, 5.6.19
12 Essay, *Deep Civilization*, BBC, 2019
13 *The Bible*, Mathew 21, Mark 13, Luke 21

15

Is There Any Hope?

Desmond Tutu, former South African bishop and theologian, once said, "Hope is being able to see that there is light despite all of the darkness."[1]

Much of our world is in darkness, as we have discussed. The future often appears hopeless. Will we ever be able to prevent pandemics or a nuclear holocaust? Is world peace ever achievable? Will the millions living in dire poverty ever find relief? Will our climate issues be solved? Is there any light amidst the darkness?

We hope so. Our very lives depend on it. The world has been through dark times before, and survived.

History is full of people who, despite life-threatening difficulties, have lived in hope, faced towards the light, and pulled through. If one has hope then anything is possible.

Movie superman, Christopher Reeve, was paralysed from the neck down following an equestrian accident. He was confined to a wheelchair and on a ventilator for the rest of his life. He said, "Once you choose hope, anything's possible."[2]

Herein lies the secret. Having hope leads to action. Having no hope leads to despair, bitterness and death. The Oxford Dictionary definition says hope is 'a feeling of expectation and desire for a particular thing to happen'. If we hope for peace, climate stability or economic equality and work towards those goals then solutions are possible. If we lack the will and there is no hope, nothing will happen.

On the global scene the same principle applies, although the challenges may often appear like mountains. Having hope, however, drives us onwards, looking for something better.

As we conclude the first quarter of the twenty-first century what do we hope for?

- We want to see an end to our climate upheavals and the huge natural disasters.
- We hope for massive advances in the use of clean, renewable energy and sustainable practices.
- We yearn for an end to wars, and the misery they bring. We desperately hope for peace.
- We hope to see a solution for the 100 million displaced persons around the globe, victims of conflicts, persecution and human rights.
- We seek gender equality, and an end to child marriage and worker exploitation.
- We hope for an end to poverty. It is estimated that 712 million people live in extreme poverty.

These are major issues, and there are many others, including cyber security, society polarisation, the spread of disinformation and political extremism. I sometimes despair at the decline of democracy around the world and the rise of authoritarianism.

I feel so powerless as I do more thinking about these massive issues. They're beyond my control. I am but one small cog at the bottom of the world, within a massive, complex global machine.

It is to be hoped that world leaders will work faster and more cleverly at solving these problems. I hope and pray that they will stop using violence to combat violence, and negotiate for peace; that they will be given wisdom and greater compassion for their fellow human beings; and that they will learn to work together.

Optimistic

While I despair at the sinful side of human nature, I'm optimistic about the creative side. Human beings have risen to great heights with their pioneering advances and innovative activities. We've found our way out of darkness in the past.

We've discovered cures for major diseases such as poliomyelitis, and ended slavery and apartheid. We have made jet aeroplanes, flown to the moon, set up space stations, discovered the computer and internet, and created the United Nations' Declaration of Human Rights. Nothing seems impossible.

My hope is that such talent will be used collectively to resolve the issues now confronting us. We created them. We can solve them. Leaving it all to the next generation is not an option.

When we look to the future there is some room for optimism but much concern about the critical challenges we face.

At the moment the global outlook doesn't look good. Over the next decade we will see a "fragmented, turbulent world order take shape", according to The World Economic Forum.[3]

Unfortunately, there is no apparent end in sight to some issues. Nuclear arsenals keep expanding. The goal of ending extreme poverty by 2030 probably won't be met. Misinformation and disinformation seem set to dominate politics for some years to come. Economic uncertainty continues to loom large.

However, the good news is that some progress is being made. There have been successful innovations to combat climate change, and breakthroughs in sustainable practices. Nuclear fusion is on the horizon. At the 2023 United Nations Climate Change Conference 118 countries agreed to triple renewable energy capacity by 2030, and, for first time, agreed to shift away from using fossil fuels, although they didn't agree to phase them out. The conference did note, however, that the world is a way behind in reducing greenhouse gases.

There have been advances in technology that will benefit humankind. The innovative mind will keep adapting to a changing world. There will be more breakthroughs. Regulated artificial intelligence will open new doors.

"We have always held to the hope, the belief, the conviction that there is a better life, a better world, beyond the horizon," said former American president, Franklin D. Roosevelt.[4]

We hope so, too.

[1] socratic-method.com
[2] https://www.setquotes.com
[3] Global Risks Perception Survey, World Economic Forum, 2024
[4] https://www.brainyquote.com

PART C

A brief thought about adapting
to change, some learnings about life
from living on this planet for over
eight decades, and a few of my books about
life, which are still available.

16
Adapt And Survive

A Japanese scholar once said, "The art of life lies in a constant readjustment to our surroundings."[1]

So true. If we want to lead full and successful lives, we have to keep adapting to what's going on around us, or we won't survive. Why? Because the world is in a continual state or flux, and we can so easily be left behind.

Change is going on all the time. It's inevitable. That's why living has become so complex. It's not just continual technological developments but changes in the workplace and careers, changes in relationships, health, transport, housing, social development – most aspects of life. If we fail to keep pace with these changes, we're in big trouble.

I remember when personal computers first came on the scene. I was hesitant to get one but am pleased I did. Now I can't do without it. I also delayed buying a cell phone, relying instead on the landline. Ongoing scam calls forced me to change. If I still tried to use the same car I possessed when in my twenties I wouldn't be able to commute as well as I do now. If

I hadn't kept abreast of new teaching techniques my career would have suffered. If I hadn't been able to cope with certain crises and challenges my life would have stagnated.

Society has changed in so many ways since the Second World War. If we fail to adapt, life can get tough.

Of course, it's natural to resist some changes, because we feel safe and secure in our present situation or because we fear the outcomes. And sometimes it's good to wait a while until the change proves to be valid or beneficial. However, if we continue to resist, we will find it difficult to survive or end up on anti-depressants.

Adapting to ongoing change, however we do so, will help us learn and grow. We will move forward in life. Psychologists readily point out that adapting makes us more resilient, and opens up greater opportunities.

I always told my students to develop their talents and skills to the fullest, while forever keeping their options open, for in their lifetimes they might have to change jobs several times, and new doors will more easily open. I'm glad I acted on my own advice, having trained for and held two professional careers and one business one. Life has been full, interesting and exciting. I've survived.

While it is true that some changes and crises will challenge us, such as the rise of artificial intelligence, we need to learn to adapt if we want to keep in step with the world around us.

George Bernard Shaw once said, "Progress is impossible without change; and those who cannot change their minds cannot change anything."[2]

---

[1] Kakuso Okakura, *The Book of Tea,* azquotes.com
[2] theinspiringjournal.com

17
Some Learnings From Life

If we want to lead a full and healthy life we need to keep thinking and learning.

When we do so, we grow and become more interesting people, able to help others more fully.

This doesn't mean we have to study for university degrees, but it does mean being alert to what is going on around us, listening and observing, keeping an open mind, and learning from the experiences of others.

Here are twelve of the many lessons I've learned from a broad and busy existence on Planet Earth.

1. Count your blessings.

    Whatever the circumstances, good or bad, it's always healthy to be thankful. Even the worst of days contain some positives, glimmers of hope. Reflect on the good moments, and be grateful.

2. Persevere

    Sometimes life can be pretty tough. We might

grieve over the loss of someone special, struggle to survive financially, be the victim of a natural disaster or assault or a terrible accident, feel lonely, experience failure...

We could feel sorry for ourselves and play the victim or face the situation head-on and be determined to work through it until we come out the other side.

Overcoming bad times requires a bit of hard work. If we fail, we must try again and again, and never give up. Success will taste all the sweeter.

3. Don't dwell on the past.

   Too often we tend to dwell on past hurts. If we want to move ahead and get the best out of life, we need to let them go. Constant revisiting past negative events can cause mental stress and hold us back.

4. Avoid worrying about the future.

   While it is good to plan ahead and work towards goals, constant worrying about what might happen will just make us anxious and sick.

5. Live in the present.

   We need to take each day as it comes. It's good to be alive. I've learnt to treasure every moment and move ahead half-a-day at a time, taking opportunities as they arise, walking through new doors as they open.

6. Accept yourself as you are, warts and all.

   No matter how we look, where we live or what we do, each one of us is a precious human being, and someone loves us and cares for us. It's not natural to try and be someone else, although we can learn from good models. Just be true to yourself.

7. Good health is our greatest asset.

   We need to look after ourselves, eating good food and keeping fit. It's difficult to fulfil the things we want to do and to serve others if we are not in good shape ourselves.

8. Use your talents to the full.

   Every human being has been gifted with, or developed, certain talents. It's vital for one's own progress, and for the benefit of those around us, to extend these as far as we can. It helps us live life to the full.

9. Make good friends.

   Friendship is invaluable for sharing life's issues and combatting loneliness. It helps to belong to a group of like-minded people who pursue something worthwhile.

10. Learn to love

    People need love and compassion, whoever they are, wherever they come from, and even if we don't like them very much. Love conquers hate.

11. Forgive

    It is difficult sometimes to forgive people who have wronged us, but if we harbour unforgiveness it will hurt us. We may never forget what happened to us, but ongoing unforgiveness simply causes unnecessary pain and frustration. It may take some courage but it will be worth it. When we release our hurt by forgiving, we will feel freer to get on with life.

12. Take time out.

    We live in an increasingly complex world. Life can be very busy. To lessen stress and maintain health it is necessary to take time to relax and reflect – to listen to some music or tune in with nature, or meditate and – think.

Also by George Bryant
Only titles of general interest are listed.

A New Society (what the Social Creditors want)

The Widening Gap (poverty in NZ)

New Zealand 2001 (published in 1981)

Beetham (biography)

The Sting in the Beehive (what Social Credit Leaders said)

The Church on Trial (conflict over social involvement)

Birthright (a story of people who care)

Twelve Plus (teenage schoolgirls)

Pathways of Hope (the story of World Vision)

George (autobiography)

New Zealand Without God?

Transformed Lives (with Bev Montgomery)

Trial to Triumph (inspiring stories of overcomers)

Way to Go (how we should live, according to Christ)

Millennium 3 (unresolved issues of our time)

Making A Real Difference (Christian movers and shakers)

Not by Might (the Graham Preston story)

Agents of Change (Kiwis making a real difference)

Life is… (reflections on life)

New Zealand 2050

Is Jesus Christ for Real?

Recent Books About Life

NEW ZEALAND 2050

Where are we heading as a nation?
What sort of people will we be?
What values will we hold?
How will we live?

What will happen to communications, farming education, health…

"Fascinating" "Stimulating" "Thought-provoking"

168pp .... RRP $26.95

LIFE IS...
An ordinary Kiwi reflects

What's life on Earth really like? Who are we? Where are we going? What are our Idols? What's the future hold? George reflects on a variety of issues vital to us all.

"Well written" – "Insightful" – "Thought-provoking" – "Sometimes provocative" – "Full of wisdom" – "Compassionate" – "Explores what it means to be human."

204pp 12 sketches .... RRP $27.95

WHY ARE WE HERE?

What in the world are human beings doing on this unique planet?

(20pp) .... RRP $5.00

WHAT IS THE MEANING OF LIFE?

Is there an overall, inherent meaning for our existence on Earth or do we just have to find our own?

(24pp) .... RRP $5.00

WHERE ARE WE GOING?

What is our future as human beings?

(24pp) .... RRP $5.00

www.ingramcontent.com/pod-product-compliance
Lightning Source LLC
Chambersburg PA
CBHW072336300426
44109CB00042B/1647